COLLEGE ADMISSIONS
OF GUILT

COLLEGE ADMISSIONS OF GUILT

HOW THE UNDERSERVED STUDENT CAN STILL SUCCEED IN HIGHER ED

NOAH JAMES T. FENSTERMACHER

NEW DEGREE PRESS

COPYRIGHT © 2021 NOAH JAMES T. FENSTERMACHER

COLLEGE ADMISSIONS OF GUILT

How the Underserved Student Can Still Succeed in Higher Ed

ISBN   978-1-63730-374-0   *Paperback*

         978-1-63730-375-7   *Kindle Ebook*

         978-1-63730-376-4   *Ebook*

CONTENTS

To My Friends, Family, and Found Family Along the Way...
Mom, Dad, Jonah, Luke, Nan, and Pap
This book is for you.
Alyssa, Annie, Nathon, Devonne, and Adam
And to all the others too numerous to list here.
Here's to all the best stories yet to be told.

ACKNOWLEDGMENTS

First and foremost, I'd like to thank my family. Mom, Dad, Jonah, Luke, Nan, and Pap. Thank you for the constant support and love. Mom, thank you for always "loving me for my brain" and helping me put it to best use. Dad, thanks for all the honest feedback and advice, especially when I needed it. And Pap, thank you for always being my number one supporter from day one.

Thank you to all my interviewees. Thank you for taking time out of your busy days to talk with me about storytelling, strategizing, and student success. Without you, this book would be lacking in personal experiences and application of ideas.

Thank you to my found family in Annie, Alyssa, Adam, Nathon, and Devonne. You supported and encouraged me throughout this whole writing process and made it all possible.

Lastly, I want to thank the New Degree Press's Eric Koester, Brian Bies, and rest of the publication crew for their incredible work in helping these cautionary tales and success stories come to light.

I'd like to acknowledge those who have given this book and the stories within it legs strong enough to move forward:

The Susquehanna University staff, Penn State admissions department, my Shikellamy school district family, and my hometown of Sunbury, Pennsylvania, for the constant support.

I'd also like to gratefully acknowledge:

Mary Lou Klotz, Jena Bogovich, Adam Guo, Nathaniel Sullivan, Keegan Myers, Lora Casteline, Jordi Comas, Caleb Stroman, Lakeisha Meyer, Lana Harris, Tre' Bohannon, Kuuipo Tom, Renee Thornton-Roop, Jon Andrew Loeliger, Gian Fabian, Tara Spencer, Marcia Slaton, Joey Wolf, Andrea Wary, Jennifer Martin, Sarah Farbo, Tiana Rawls-White, Carly Salter, Sandra Feather, Matthew Santa, Lindsay Granquist, Angela Gemberling, Stacy St. James, Leah Weinberg, Penn Garvin, Jacob Bubeck, Darius Williams-McKenzie, Jena Lui, Matt & Tammy Foltz, Shelby Laudenslager, Jared Geise, Rachel Foulds, Julie Ritchie Wagner, Lenaire Ahlum, Dakota Zimmerman, Robert Long, Cecelia Shellenberger, Matt Spade, Frank Fleming, Sydney Keister, Larry Wary, Jodie Hogan, Melissa Byers, Kristine Rosancrans, Shanon Benjamin, Craig Stark, Cara Morgan, Carter May, Keith Spencer, Steven Stumbris, Tom Moran, Stephenie Wolf, Taneja Williams, Matt Barone, Heidi Mackey, Madilyn Brosious, Nicole Kalcich, Sue Roshoe, Valerie Smith-Gonzalez, Lauren Gooch, Shelley Moyer, Anna Ivey, Basil Mokhallalati, Renee Austin, Ingrid Colt, Jessica Walters, Ryan Carter, Michaeline Shuman, Angelique Poragratti, Aaron Rill, Ginny Motyka, Tessa Redina, Kathy Hastings, Eric Koester, MaKayla Keister, Dana Miville, Robert Springall, Jordan Garrigan, Meghan Beck, Erin Kenney, Sherri Scholl, Jennifer Rager-Kay, Cindy McDaniels, Kate Kishbaugh, Sherri Metcalfe, Margaux Murray, Jerica Shuck, Mike Makowsky, Cari Hallman, Angela

Hummel, Jennifer Hauf, Robert Sieczkiewicz, Isaac Conner, Sabrina Burger, LaNysha Foss, and Rebecca Schell.

Lastly, I'd like to acknowledge a few sources of inspiration: Mackenzie Fierceton, Devonte White, Samyr Qureshi, LaWanda Ward, Dana Budzyn, David Guthrie, Cheryl Strumpf, Dr. Stacey Pearson-Wharton, Dr. Towuanna Porter-Brannon, Charles Cotton, Edward Zayas, Jr., and President Jonathan Green.

INTRODUCTION: WHY STUDENTS MUST MASTER STRATEGIC STORYTELLING

———

Never judge a book by its cover...unless you like this cover—then judge away.

It often feels like that's what we do in college admissions. We scratch the surface of somebody's story before stamping decisions that shape their lives. It makes you wonder: Whose story sells? Whose "book" gets bought, and better yet, how do they catch a college's curiosity? As a first-generation college student, I'm working toward our generation being the last to ask these questions.

My book's cover reads, "lower income, nonwhite, blue-collar," and for some, that's where they stop reading. And I get it, the promising high school athlete predicts a promising career at a Division I school and the straight-A student heads straight to the Ivy League. But me? I'm not so sure. Folks might not get to the part where the student who claimed he'd "never use this math in the real world" became an entrepreneur in the education field.

I've worked as assistant producer for the *Being the Dot* podcast that amplifies voices of students of color at predominantly white institutions. I've started making a mobile app that better translates what a campus's climate and culture are like for prospective students. A film is in the works on the school-to-prison pipeline. And there's a new community college being created in my home of Susquehanna Valley in part due to my being on its board of directors. All of this I accomplished before my twenty-third birthday, an aspect I highlight at the start of my paid public speaking engagements.

This isn't me patting myself on the back either; it's proof of concept: *strategic storytelling makes stories that sell.*

Mackenzie Fierceton understands this. A University of Pennsylvania graduate, she aged out of foster care, experienced homelessness throughout high school, and went on to study at Oxford (Ozio,Ron). She was also nominated for the world's most prestigious international Rhodes Scholarship, of which other recipients include US President Bill Clinton, Director of the US Domestic Policy Council Susan Rice, and sitting Senator Corey Booker. Her advice she gave me in an interview?

"Don't reduce me to poverty porn."

While often read as a chronicle of rags-to-riches, she asserts it was knowing *how* to tell her story, utilizing said experience, and then funneling that toward her research into the foster-care-to-prison pipeline that she won the scholarship for. Her firsthand knowledge, academic record, and storytelling ability allowed her to navigate the hierarchies of higher education to make a difference. This difference, she states, makes *all* the difference in terms of charting one's path in life.

See, American universities suffer from what can best be described as *narrative gentrification.* The dominant discourse asserts that honors students, AP classes, and elite institutions lead to great success and that everyone has an equal chance of attaining it. The counter-narrative that runs opposite of this takes into account the **achievement gap**: the array of academic outcomes between the affluent and the impoverished. The conversation now includes other **intrinsic characteristics** students may not have chosen but still have significant impact on their life. Their race, religion, and other identifiers also relate to their school experience (Abaramson, 2018).

It is true the best predictor of future achievement is past achievement, but when some students are given opportunities for success others are not, it then becomes a question of said opportunities—an **opportunity gap**—one that must be resolved through **access** and **resources** made available to all. The Glossary of Education Reform defines *access* as the ways in which educational institutions and policies ensure—or at least strive to ensure—students have equitable opportunities to take full advantage of their education. To do that, one needs *resources*, or the means and/or services in which that accessibility can be provided.

But you haven't been told about this, have you?

Nigerian author and TEDx Talk speaker Chimamanda Ngozi Adichie makes mention of "the dangers of a single story," noting we risk a critical misunderstanding when we lack a diverse perspective (Adiche, 2009). Growing up, my dad used to tell me if one person called you an ass, you ignore them. If two do so, you consider it. After three, you'd best buy a saddle. While less eloquent and more folksy, there is an assuredness that many stories conveying the same message may have some truth to them.

So, when 75.3 percent of first-generation students predict they'll need to find work during their freshman year, it's a story worth telling. And when less than 50 percent of first-generation students are likely to graduate on time, we need to listen for why. How about the 1.6 million students attending a school with sworn law enforcement officers, but not a school counselor? And especially the dropout rates of sixteen to twenty-four-year-old students who come from low-income families that are seven times more likely to drop out than those from families with higher incomes (Jacimovic, 2021).

It's the story of how a foster care kid overcomes the complications of a hectic home life, which she transforms into valuable intelligence toward what she wants to do with her life and convinces others to do the same. Fierceton asks, "What can I do so that others like me can succeed?"

Treating people fairly can mean treating people differently.

Equality is focused on an even distribution of treatment, ignoring the situational factors of some members of a group so no one is given any differing sort of attention. So those that need don't receive, and those that are fine do better over time.

Equity is fairness based on attention to individuals, personalizing students' education based on a needs-focused framing. In this model, students attain the access they need, so those that need will receive, and those that are fine continue to do just fine! Equity is not like a pie; no one is "giving up their piece" to allow for the proper treatment of other students (*Thinking Maps*, 2019).

A simple concept, yeah? I thought so too, even as I became an admissions professional and saw past the clean cover of college admissions brochures to the fine print that paints a picture of preference for certain students over others. Criminal conspiracies like the 2019 admissions bribery scandal center on coconspirators scamming their kids' way into the Ivies, implying some dragon's hoard of intellectual wealth to be acquired.

What they must not know, that I now know, is that you can get into the Ivy League and come out with an expensive diploma and an even more expensive loan, or find that a community college close to home strikes closer to gold. While metaphorical, if community colleges created the likes of Morgan Freeman, George Lucas, and Steve Jobs, I wouldn't write them off just yet (Sisloak, 2017). I remember a higher-up bringing the team together before another college admission season explicitly telling us, "We are assessors, not advocates."

I remember asking, "What if we should? What if we should advocate *as* we assess? Not tipping the scales by any means, just looking at admissions in a different way. We could change the idea of what a successful student could look like—"

And I remember being sharply told admissions remains color-blind for a reason—*equality*. And that I shouldn't let my *skin color* blind me to what my job is.

I didn't have the words then, so I'll write them out now: *the college admissions process is equal, but not equitable.*

As James Baldwin states, not everything faced can be changed, but nothing can be changed until it's faced. It's as true as his other advice, in that people are trapped in history as much as history is trapped in them. But here's a word of advice from me: the story is not just important in that it's being told, but in how it is told. What if we could repackage those experiences, those inequities, and those challenges you've overcome from a problem to a positive?

This is **strategic storytelling**: the best way for the underrepresented student to best represent themselves. This is that story, *our* story, as you learn and add your own lived experience to it. For many, it's a case of the ill-informed misinforming the uninformed, and we're here to break that vicious cycle. The fact is, we as humans care more about stories over statistics and names over numbers. I've compiled the success stories and cautionary tales of college presidents, Forbes listers, and award-winning educators into one college prep material to help guide college students and college students-to-be on how to navigate the halls of higher education.

When life gets hard, don't close the book; just turn the page. If you too want to learn how to catch colleges' attention, create the campus experience you want, and become accomplished well beyond the classroom, I invite you to do the same.

HOW TO USE THIS BOOK

A good education is a foundation for a better future

ELIZABETH WARREN

We've heard all the common advice. Visit a variety of different schools, even if you're not interested in applying there, to see for yourself what fits for you. This gives a reference to what you will like/dislike. Stay overnight if you can to see comfortability as much as compatibility. Have a "dream" and a "safety" school. This is all about finding your fit.

Your fit.

Whenever I heard that I couldn't help but chuckle, as if I were a square with equal sides searching for the space I'd slip perfectly into. It isn't like the children's toys, with the shapes with holes made just for them. It's like a puzzle of pieces, some missing, and no picture to see what it's supposed to be. Me? I've felt this way all my life.

Little did I know looking to find your "fit" can take away the possibility of contributing something that's not yet there that everybody needs. Instead of looking for environments that fit, know your values and the aspects of a cultural community you want, and don't be afraid of adding something new. Some ideas need to be challenged, and that's a story in and of itself.

The end of one story is the start of another, your high school graduation being a perfect example. You're leaving behind your childhood, lifelong friends, and the classes where you still had to ask to use the restroom. This is the big leagues now, the real world, and you can use the bathroom whenever you want.

But over half a decade ago, I didn't know then what I know now, and had the same questions circling around that might be spinning in your head.

How do I stand out on college applications?

When will I know I've chosen the right school?

Am I ready for college?

College readiness looks different for everybody. While traditionally tied to institutional aid and certain academic marks conventionally geared toward what student success looks like, life factors contribute to one's performance in other areas of life. While one student may look more "college ready" over another, taking a more holistic view gives a more accurate estimation of their educational competence.

This book will be your reference material for any and all things concerning "college readiness," which could more accurately be described as **college preparedness.** Those unaware of the "proper" terminology aren't "not ready" for college, just less prepared than someone who does have them. For example, if you're a prospective student sweating over some college applications right now, here are some words you might want to know:

TEN WORDS TO KNOW BEFORE YOU GO

1. *Major:* This is the reason you came to college—your area of interest that you'll be taking classes in. It could be English, engineering, or aeronautics, and all that you do will tie back to ensuring you're ready to enter the workforce with the needed skills for it. You can also minor in another field of interest and accrue credit for those courses taken as well. For example, one could major in marketing and minor in communications.

2. *Semester:* Your first semester on campus will typically be your fall semester, ranging from the end of August to the middle of December. A second semester will start mid-January, your Spring semester, and last until mid-May. Each will be approximately fifteen weeks long, with a possible summer term available for those interested in taking additional classes.

3. *Syllabus:* This serves as your guideline to each college class, one that is typically read or advised to read before the first class that outlines expectations and assignments. The *course number* will also be here, something you can also look up online when you register for a course.

4. *Prerequisite:* While on the subject of classes, some will be "prerequisite," meaning they must be completed before you're able to advance to a higher-level course. You'll take several during your first year on campus, many of them *general education courses* that center on a range of more basic concepts rather than the more specialized classes you'll take specifically for your major.

5. *Credit Hour:* This denotes how many hours a week you'll physically dedicate to the class. This number, along with all the other credit hours you'll have per semester, determines your full- or part-time student status.

6. *Bachelor's degree:* This is what you'll earn by the end of your typical four-year journey at your undergraduate institution. Associate's degrees are usually two years' worth of study, with your academic year taking the place of your "grade" from high school. Instead of being in eleventh or twelfth grade, you'll start off as a first-year, then second-year, and so on and so forth.

7. *Extracurricular:* Similar to high school, extracurriculars are the activities that encompass your time when you're not in school or at work. They can include club sports, intramurals, and organizations such as Greek life. Greek life refers to fraternities and sororities, generally single-gender social groups that commit to community service events and recreational fun.

8. *Internship:* Speaking of, while on campus, you can look for paid or unpaid positions related to your field of study and possibly receive credit upon completion, called an internship. These can be especially helpful in securing a position out of college.

9. *Office hours:* I know this is a lot, so don't be afraid to locate mentors at your university. Office hours refer to the times in which professors and other professionals on campus are open to receiving students' questions and drop-ins. These hours are also included on the course syllabus for professors. You'll be assigned an adviser, someone on campus in a professional capacity that will be your go-to for all things guidance. They will also send you their hours of availability.

10. *Student affairs:* This will be the specific subset of professionals on campus involved with your campus journey. From student life offices to residential life departments,

they will facilitate your college experience from day one until the day you cross that stage for your diploma.

This book will also provide:

ADVICE FROM THE EXPERTS

I recently interviewed Gaelle Pierre-Louis, Harvard graduate and Georgetown admissions officer, who blew my mind when we talked finances.

"You served on the Fulbright Committee, you're part of the Harvard Black Alumni Society, and you've written a whole book about it. You're incredible!" I told her during our interview. "What's some advice on understanding the college admissions process?"

Her answer?

1. *Financial aid departments* are where colleges determine money given on the basis of need, with the practice in place for students academically qualified but perhaps lacking the funds to pursue higher education. Reaching out to specific colleges you're applying to will help immensely, as there are entire departments set up to handle these affairs and sort yours out too.

2. *Merit-based scholarships* are based not upon need, but athletic, academic, or artistic ability. Collegenet.com and Scholarships.com are both reliable resources for these opportunities, which can be anywhere from a few hundred to a few thousand dollars! When you hear about the football star getting a "free-ride" to school, this can be what they're referring to, with some scholarships paying your entire way through college.

3. *Renegotiating prices!* This is the one that sent me. Did you know colleges and used-car dealerships had so much in

common? An oversimplification, sure, but not without merit (pun intended). There is a difference between the *sticker price* and the *net price*. The sticker price of a university is what you read online—the one your parents read and have mini heart attacks over. Thankfully, the net price is the actual price you pay once all your financial aid and merit-based scholarships are given out. To give you a frame of reference, I did reasonably well in school, and my undergraduate institution gave me a scholarship that cut my tuition for all four years in half! I mean, there was still a big bill to pay, but it goes to show what you see on screen and what you pay at the end of the day are hopefully two very different numbers.

In fact, I spoke with a host of admissions counselors, all with their own easy-to-implement advice. "Be your own advocate," says Professor Paul Umbach of North Carolina State University.

"We can't blame lower-income students for the financial situations we find ourselves in, but we can take every measure to increase our odds at future success."

Umbach also serves as principal for Percontor, an educational research and training company. He specifically studies what factors go into increasing a student's ability to continue their education. While we have our own experiences, we think it's best to consult the experts like the professor and Chris Lombardo.

Chris is a former CollegeVine consultant, one of the nation's top college advising organizations (for free!), where he gained insight into multiple aspects of college admissions; he served as an individual tutoring consultant for high school juniors and seniors on the admissions application process for six months. This was in addition to managing teams of people and organizing curriculum resources. His advice?

"Don't look at [college admissions] as something to game… Figure out what you're interested in (in high school) and be involved in them early: join clubs, hobbies, skills, etc. Try a wide variety, especially if you do not know what you want to study or what you are interested in. Later, when realities of admissions process are more present, you will handle it much easier."

Writing is a large portion of the admissions process, according to Chris, especially for more competitive schools, which require well-written essays. Even in a STEM-related field, being able to write and communicate effectively is important. Showing you can through activities or self-started projects can be a huge advantage in honing your skills.

And Chris knows all about a well-written essay. He graduated from Cornell with a degree in physics and then an English literature degree in 2018. After finding work at a creative writing program at Northwestern, Chris pursued a dual degree in English literature and creative writing. It's unsurprising Chris is striving to be a professor in creative writing and a fiction writer.

Even if you're not looking to be a bestselling author, Chris advises you sharpen up those soft skills. And Professor Umbach? Thanks to him, we have facts-based challenges and benefits students, especially lower-income students, should be aware of:

CHALLENGES & BENEFITS

CHALLENGES

- Access to Resources

    "It's a very complicated process, and the information and networks high school students have are under resourced. For example, there's a week in November where private universities in my area waive application fees, so having someone 'in the know' is definitely helpful!"

    PAUL D. UMBACH

- Useful mentors

    "In lower-income schools, counselor-to-student ratio needs improvement, depleting counseling access for inexperienced families with the college process. If your school is underfunded and lacking in mentor figures, do be sure to look up organizations (PCAC, NACAC, etc.).

    PAUL D. UMBACH

- Financial Literacy

    "Understand college costs, especially how to apply for financial aid. Know the difference between 'sticker price,' what you might find online, and the 'net price' that you actually pay after scholarships, loans, and other monetary rewards for academic effort."

    PAUL D. UMBACH

BENEFITS

- Assistance given to students

> *"Organizations like the College Advising Corps and the Near Peers program bridge the gap between what lower-income students know and don't know. There's evidence this works. Events like College Application Week, [and] financial literacy websites that walk families through the process are all incredibly insightful.*
>
> PAUL D. UMBACH

Thanks to our expert advice, we've even laid out a four-year plan for high schoolers to track their progress in the applications process. This is by no means a blueprint of how it *should* work, but as a guideline for those who do better with a little direction.

FOUR-YEAR WALKTHROUGH

———

High school can be hard. It's the last stop for many folks before the "real world"—whatever that means—but also the last preparatory phase before higher education for those interested. These last few teachers, classes, and extracurriculars will serve as your resumes and recommendations moving forward. It's a lot to take in, and you might be bombarded with a well-meaning but irritating slew of questions from concerned parties.

Where are you going to college? You should go here/there. What're you studying? No, study this instead of that. Is there even any money in your field?

Do you have this done yet? Oh, well you better!

School's stressful enough, so what we've compiled is a guided walkthrough of what your high school experience, at any stage, can really look like. Again, this does not mean you have to follow every aspect, but if you're a little lost, there's no harm in looking through some advice.

FRESHMAN YEAR

This year is not as much concrete as it is abstract. Test out your areas of interest. Take the PSAT (Practice Standardized Scholastic Assessment Test) and AP (Advanced Proficient) classes if available/financially viable within your academic skill set range. Honors classes that challenge you also are persuasive on applications.

SOPHOMORE YEAR

This year is similar to your freshman year, just escalated. For example, learn from current club leaders about how to run for managing positions in groups, found your own clubs, and take initiative in what you're passionate about. Lay the groundwork for junior year to be your "shining star."

JUNIOR YEAR

This year is the most important in building your application since the cutoff for most application deadlines is the end of junior year. It's the last "full year" to show how committed/ successful you are.

Complete the SAT and other standardized tests. Before, you won't know all the material, and by senior year, you may have too much going on. Decide where you want to apply so your senior year is all about focusing on getting there. Decide if you want urban/rural, small/large; then senior year is all about finding the specific school you want.

SENIOR YEAR

The actual admissions process: Open availability starts in August, including the Common Application essay. You'll have the most deadlines for essays, recommendations, and completing applications from August to December. Be sure to ask teachers/employers well in advance to give them time. If you wait until the last minute to ask, you'll get a last-minute response, and they're typically not as thought out as one they've taken weeks to think over and choose their wording carefully. The best people to ask are your junior/senior year teachers. Go on physical/virtual tours when possible.

How do I stand out at X University?

Honestly, it depends on the person and their academic interest. Students typically approach college applications with their specialization in mind: Dedicate yourself to a certain identity marker. Show a passion that lets colleges know you are an impassioned student and be sure to include a "hook" that draws them in to want to read more. Get away from idea that you're well rounded and become more specialized as a student.

When will I know I've chosen the right school?

On campus tours: Take notes, especially as a sophomore, because you're not going to remember these things. Take advantage of the time you're physically on campus to talk with a student. Students could be in similar major to what you're pursuing and give inside info on campus life. They're often reliable, unbiased sources of info.

We're discussing the on-paper principles of brick-and-mortar institutions, easily accessible information to the public and what their websites will proudly proclaim. Before I got accepted, I'd never known about the **hidden curriculum** of colleges—the norms and values of an academic environment not covered in the course syllabus.

Am I ready for college?

You can look at SAT or GPA scores to measure compatibility with a school. Even with a lower score, it doesn't mean you are out of the race, so to speak. A number of universities use a holistic approach to admissions, making a decision based on *all* the information you've given them (hence the guideline for high school above).

But the best way to be sure? Keep reading. There's a deeper story here involving an over $25-million-money-laundering scheme with heavy implications on your future endeavors.

BIASED ON A TRUE STORY

———

Lower-income first-generation students of color: I hear you. If it seems like the odds are against you, I'd be lying if I didn't say that wasn't by design. Since Harvard was founded, the bastions of knowledge were a haven for the haves, not the have-nots. To compete, you'll need to plan for upward mobility and lots of lateral movement.

Upward mobility is why you're at college; you get the degree to get the job you might not have had the opportunity for without the degree. Especially for underprivileged students, the monetary and "social station" aspect can be enticing, encouraging students who might not have enjoyed school to do what's best for them to earn more down the line.

Lateral movement is really career maneuverability, wherein you can have options once you graduate and don't feel stuck on one path or without anywhere to go.

But why do underprivileged students even *need* to do all the extra work? Well, it's a long story but I'll keep it quick.

During my very short tenure in undergraduate public relations, word about a criminal conspiracy surrounding Yale, Stanford, and other top-tier schools was spreading. What would come to be known as the 2019 college admissions bribery scandal was just a whisper in 2018, two years before my graduation.

Lori Loughlin, best known for her *Full House* role as Rebecca, was indicted as one of the thirty-three parents involved in the scandal. Loughlin was charged with paying over $20 million to inflate her kids' SAT scores and then bribe the enrollment professionals. The SAT, or Scholastic Assessment Test, is the standardized exam acting as the gateway to college admissions. Administered by the educational testing service aptly called the College Board, these 157 questions (and optional essay portion) are the great equalizer to emphasize one's fitness for graduate study.

Except that it isn't.

To understand just how much Loughlin fixed the system into her favor, we first have to understand it. The SAT is $49.50 alone; the price jacks up to $64.50 with the addition of the essay portion. You obviously want to study for this all-important exam, so you'll be out of another fifty dollars for an "inexpensive" prep book. That's right; you can't just study class materials or look for it online. There's a special booklet with the specific ideas covered on the exam, and if you want a competitive score, it comes separately.

But fine, you think. We're at $114.15 tops—impracticable but manageable. Now it'll cost you just another $11.15 to send out said scores to your schools of choice... each. If you're thinking of applying to multiple schools, you'd best be thinking on it with deep pockets. Still, you've watched your hard-earned money get gobbled in the test-making, money-grabbing machine that will churn out your diploma, hopefully, and so you bite the bullet on this one.

Except.

Folks like Loughlin, and the thirty-two other parents involved in what would be one of the largest conspiracies to commit mail fraud the US Justice Department has ever prosecuted. In fact, William Rick Singer, the scheme's organizer, ran a nonprofit called Key Worldwide Foundation. Their mission? To provide quality access to education for underprivileged youth (Reilly, 2020).

In short, a man tasked with making education more equitable unethically accepted million-dollar bribes to help the well off get away with honest services fraud. While you scrounged to afford a chance at continued education, someone else made sure all that was in vain, and *that* is why educational equity is so important. Codenamed Operation Varsity Blues—yes, from the film of the same name—FBI agents infiltrated the crime ring and exposed its participants, unwittingly also shedding light on how the standardized assessment algorithm needed fixing.

Stories like Loughlin's are unfortunately not unique. In 2019, Harvard legally defended itself in *Students for Fair Admissions v. Harvard,* a lawsuit from rejected Asian-American applicants citing a "racial quota" as reasons for why they were denied entry into the esteemed institution. Harvard, too? Even the political minefield merged with higher education; 2020 presidential candidates Elizabeth Warren and Cory Booker both attached themselves to movements that called for student loan relief (Lockhart, P.R.).

But it's not all backroom bribes and school scandals. People want pulp fiction and sensationalized stories when the truth is much harder to stomach; this is systemic. I gave you the above example about the SAT as an exception, not the rule. Most folks can't afford to throw money at their problems, and so one can wave that off as an outlier.

Except.

Consider the College Board's abandoned attempt at acknowledging adversity through its adversity scores, a concept meant to codify and then quantify the lived experiences of particularly underprivileged individuals into a single number. While well intentioned, it had the unintended effect of inciting an "oppression Olympics" of sorts, commercializing and capitalizing on the discrimination faced by applicants.

Also consider early decision practices that are *binding*, meaning, if you apply and get accepted, that's it—you're in, without a choice. You are forced to attend the university, and by doing so, lock out your chances of applying elsewhere. This is not necessarily bad, especially if that's your dream school, right? Don't forget a college is a company, with a bottom line like any other business, and guaranteeing a number of students' tuition guarantees it will meet its quota for that academic year, and so can be more selective when regular admissions season rolls around.

The folks that don't need financial aid packages benefit, while others wait for offers of assistance. And once that yearly quota is met, selectivity can ensue over who else can attend the prestigious school. This is simple supply and demand economics. For early decision, commitment is key, while the rest wait outside locked gates hoping for another chance in.

I looked for other ways higher education offers financial aid to its student populace and found the hundreds of thousands of dollars given away as scholarships for interactive, competitive video gaming at the collegiate level: e-sports. I met with Juniata College's e-sports director, Alex Kurtz, who brought up the concepts of skill floor and ceiling during our interview.

Skill floor refers to the base level of attributes needed to successfully navigate an experience effectively, or the "you must be this tall to ride" of the real world. **Skill ceilings** are the maximum level of potential for an interaction, like how the dream of every Division I football player is to find themselves playing in the Super Bowl. "Not everyone can afford going to college," Kurtz said. "So if we can solve some money problems *and* incentivize them to join our program, it's a win-win!" *That's* equitable education.

Bringing it back to testing, the financial skill floor for the SAT is being able to afford the prep book, the test itself, and the fee to send it to all the schools you want to apply to. The skill ceiling is being able to have the funds to literally bend the system your way, bribing people in positions of power to inflate scores and push your application through. Sadly, even if you're not movie star famous, folks privileged enough to afford the more thorough prep books or hire an in-person tutor specifically for the SAT can dramatically increase their chances at achieving higher marks. By one measure (financial) alone, the high skill floor of the SAT can make the college application process improbable. *If I can't handle this, why even go on?*

Offering a wider window for waiving fees on SAT scores is a start, but why even have a separate prep book families are forced to buy for one-time use? Instead, incorporate prep classes that cover the same materials in high school, an elective for those that want to do well on the exam but aren't in a financial position to purchase their way there. Oh, and scholarships that reduce the overall cost of going to college itself, even if not to play video games competitively, is another step in the right direction.

Across the nation, 1,600 schools have currently changed their application statuses to "test-optional," meaning they no longer require the SAT for admissions purposes. COVID-19 famously cancelled all SAT sessions for the 2020-21 academic year, forcing all American universities to become test optional, if even for one year, and sparking debate over whether reversing this decision post pandemic would be ethical. The College Board insists its test is the best predictor of post-graduate success, though studies have mixed reception for how events like Varsity Blues will change the game moving forward (Moody, 2018).

And if that idea frustrates you, then you'll understand why it lit a fire under me. The admissions scandal stoked those sparks that make us light up doing the things we love. I want to understand how this happened, so it never happens again. Maybe I took it more personally, being the son of a custodian and a concrete mixer-driver who saved every penny they didn't have. Anything I paid for, I'd worked for, starting as soon as I could at fifteen, and to know someone else cheated their way up has and always will always rub me the wrong way.

Still, for every story, there's a takeaway, and in our case, five factors that relate to any forward momentum you'll want.

THE FIVE FACTORS OF FORWARD MOMENTUM

———

IT'S NOT THE BRAND NAME THAT'S IMPORTANT, BUT THE BRAND BEHIND YOUR NAME THAT IS.
It's not about the name of the school on your diploma once you get it but the fact that *you got it.* You graduated with a degree, a piece of paper letting employers know you are well versed in your craft and that their company would be all the better having you join it.

It's tough to break the social conditioning that makes folks believe only eight schools along the eastern coastline are worth going to, but that's why we include stories like Fierceton and Dr. Devonte White, who you'll learn interned with the Federal Bureau of Investigation's Human Trafficking & Civil Rights Division. Did you know the FBI even had internships? Dr. White is the poster child for finding opportunities in the strangest of places and will help you understand how to be the student that sees how every conventionally closed door may have a window (of opportunity) for some unconventional experience.

COLLEGES COLLECT SOCIAL CAPITAL, SO START STOCKPILING.

Big schools mean big bucks and even bigger dreams for the students that go there, right? This is mostly true. The science behind our everyday social interactions highlights how building social capital, from high school to college and beyond, can have an even greater impact than where we went for a degree. Have you heard, *"It's who you know?"* Studies show it's a combination of who and what you know that creates the perfect measure of your rates of success in your area of interest.

According to him, Forbes 30 Under 30-lister Samyr Qureshi wouldn't have been able to create Knack without storing up social capital, a student success technology platform and peer mentoring program with the University of Florida. In addition, we wouldn't have cofounder and CEO of Universal Basic Data Income, a company concerned with ensuring US citizens' private information remains so. You'll learn how to network more effectively, tell your story on paper and in person impressively, and widen that circle to include a few famous friends!

CULTURAL CURRENCY CREATES OPPORTUNITY.

Financial literacy is enormously important when understanding possible college loan debt, the cost of living wherever you go, and how to manage money on a monthly basis. Warren Buffett, the CEO of Berkshire Hathaway (which owns several well-known companies like The Coca-Cola Company, Dairy Queen, GEICO, Bank of America, and Apple) asserts, "If you don't find a way to make money while you sleep, you'll work till you die" (Campbell).

While not as extreme, we'll dive into how you can create active and passive income, get a leg up on those student loan bills, and even position yourself for a higher-paying job once you graduate! We'll talk how to make moves and money as a "poor" college student, switching up the stereotypes to take advantage of the rich opportunities being on campus can afford.

YOUR MIND'S THE MUSCLE THAT MATTERS MOST.

Okay, so maybe the brain's not a muscle, but it flows better! You'll remember it, and that's important. Impaired by imposter syndrome? Breaking down over academic burnout? Therapist Cheryl Strumpf serves as the voice of the counselor, teaching you the correct coping strategies, tips, and warnings for student life success, and Dr. Stacey Pearson-Wharton backs her up with solid advice on navigating the uncomfortable spaces that come with coming of age on campus.

"OWN UP" WITH AN OWNERSHIP MINDSET

It can sometimes be too easy for the impoverished student to fall into this mindset. This **fixed mindset** refers to our belief our skills and abilities are static, or unchanging, and what we are born with or have naturally is all we can accomplish. Of course, as an educator, I agree with the growth approach, and encourage you to do the same. Dr. Carol Dweck of Stanford, a psychology professor, is credited for coining the term *growth mindset* and depicts it heavily in her book *Mindset: The New Psychology of Success*. Having a **growth mindset** is great, in that you constantly improve yourself and actively work toward your goals. Examples include:

- taking criticism as constructive to build upon less-developed areas,

- improving one's ability to learn new things and adapt, as well as
- seeing tasks assigned as opportunities for insight

However, the growth mindset works best when we take into account one's roots, meaning the origins of their ideas and perspectives. We have no idea about the experiences underrepresented students deal with, including but not limited to systemic oppression, food insecurity, and economic hardships. These and other life factors result in some developing a fixed mindset that is not impossible to grow into something more, but must be taken into account as the roots of what will grow in its place. We need an **ownership mindset.**

It's often utilized in twelve-step programs and other self-help initiatives, and we'll definitely need to "own up" to our past mistakes as well as what we want our future to be if we are to succeed in our scholarly pursuits. In school, you are taught a lesson before given a test.

In life, we are often tested, and *that's* what teaches us lessons.

THE STORY METHOD

At this point, practical advice replaces platitude.

How many times have we heard empty platitudes when we ask for advice, or even when we don't ask? Telling a student who worries about getting into their dream school that *"Whatever will be, will be"* doesn't help. Neither does stating *"Sometimes bad things lead to good thing"s* if they don't get in. As an admissions professional at a Pennsylvanian state school, I see where their sights are at, and who they're on. More importantly, I see who they're *not* on.

What we don't need now are parables of generations past, of people pulled up by their own bootstraps. You know where that comes from, right? Some sources cite German folklore where a wily trickster finds himself in muddied water, literally lifting himself out of the muck by, you guessed it, his own bootstraps. Another account attributes it to an early 1800s physics textbook that asked the very question of why a man could not, in fact, physically pull himself up by his bootstraps. It's a funny phrase that found itself transformed into a fast response for why the kids of today should just shut up and "work hard" for what they want and "not ask for handouts" (Zafarris).

We're literally holding ourselves to an impossible standard, and that's just one pain point to discuss.

A **pain point** is a spot of trouble that is a result of something or from something else.

For our collegiate conversation, think of pain points like:

- The cost of college
- The admissions process
- The practicality of the lessons

Here we have one example (cost of college), being a result of the high tuition rates of universities, another example (admissions process) being frustrating due to its complex procedure, and a third example (practicality), whose question remains open ended. The simplest solution to a high price is to lower it, though this is not easy. My seventh-grade English teacher had an admirable mantra she lived by, wise words she'd often start the day off with as a gentle reminder:

LIFE IS PAIN!

MRS. MURRAY

I think that's a *Princess Bride* quote. She was that teacher, the one you remember years later and reference as life changing, because while often said in jest, the thread running through her lessons was that life was inherently unfair—that the real world didn't always operate as it should and to not always expect the wheels of change to turn in your favor. Although not phrased as friendly, she meant for us to toughen up for a world that would be tough to us. And heck, as an English teacher, she knew better than most: **all good stories have conflict, and the stories of our lives are no different.**

Remember when I asked about whose book gets bought in college admissions? We can't speed read through everyone's adventures, so we inevitably seek out shortcuts to our solutions. "Mark Cuban: Power and Money," the eighth episode in the eighth season of *Brain Games*, features memory champion Nelson Dellis teaching the Dallas Mavericks owner how best to categorize mass amounts of information, presenting him with rows of people holding different colored cards. Mark was tasked with turning around and reciting the order of people holding said cards and their corresponding colors. Though about fifty in number, the American entrepreneur, with surprising simplicity, recited the order of the cards perfectly. How'd he do it?

He used the Link or *Story* Method.

Dellis described his winning strategy as, "linking information from one item to the next, creating one connected, cohesive story for easy recall later on."

A story is just a creative and engaging means of conveying information, and we're going to build off that here. If admissions counselors can't process all the data they sort through, and forget a lot from even that, you're going to need to stand out. Your interviews, resume, essays, and letters of recommendation all serve as excerpts of your story, a sneak peek into what makes you unique for universities.

Most, if not all competitive applicants, and by that I mean "in the running to actually attend the institution," have a high GPA, stellar test scores, and raving recommendation letters (because who else would you ask *except* someone who'd rave about you?). In short, unless you've got that genius GPA and a perfect SAT score, you might as well put that aside for now. We'll cover studying habits later, so let's assume your grades are as good as the next person's grades, effectively canceling that out, and leaving us with the three Es:

- Experience
- Extracurriculars
- Entrance Essay

That last one technically makes it four e's, but you get the point: This is where character is created, your personality shines through, and your **personal brand** is put on display. Your brand is how you define and promote yourself, an intangible collection of all the things you've done or said that inform how others view you. It's your reputation, your attitude, outlook on life, and, if you'll indulge me for a second, the aura you emanate to those around you.

Do you ever meet with people with such *warm* smiles, *bright* eyes, and a *welcoming* nature? Sure, they might have nice teeth and pretty eyes, which help, but their demeanor, the way they treat the world, is how we view them. Someone unfriendly but smart might be described as *cold, calculating,* and *robotic.* These don't exactly denote somebody you'd be friends with, now do they?

It's like Gandhi said:

> *"Your beliefs become your thoughts*
> *Your thoughts become your words,*
> *Your words become your actions,*
> *Your actions become your habits,*
> *Your habits become your values,*
> *Your values become your destiny."*

In short, be mindful of every little thing you do, as they become your brand, your story. As we're about to go over, that brand can be the literal difference between acceptance or rejection at a university. See, colleges are companies, and companies create products. The *telos* of higher education, their ultimate objective, is to produce graduates—employable, admirable, capable graduates, ready and willing to take on whatever challenges are thrown their way with applicable knowledge and a can-do attitude.

But in order to be that, they've got to be likable. They've got to have a **winning personality,** meaning a college can take a healthy chance on you being a "winner" out in the real world, and will positively build upon their established brand. Why does everyone want to go Harvard? It's in the Ivy League, is the nation's oldest campus, and just look at their list of successful alumni: Bill Gates, Neil deGrasse Tyson, and the late, great Ruth Bader Ginsberg all graduated from the school. Facebook founder Mark Zuckerberg didn't even graduate from there but *still* gets the recognition!

It all says the same thing: go to Harvard if you want to be a somebody. If everyone has similar scores, it comes down to those three Es that define exactly who you are, and why a top-tier college would take the chance on you. Will you embody the school's brand? Upon graduation, will you become a success story that can be further used to bring in other bold and bright young minds? While we're not here to get into Harvard specifically, we can break down how best to build your personal brand to wow college admissions professionals.

First, *control what you can control.* A few standout achievements that look good on anyone's **academic profile,** the total sum of all you've accomplished in school, are:
- Demonstration of leadership potential
- Showing interest in school of choice and career
- Take initiative towards those ends

Before you try to promote your "book" to schools, you need a basic idea of what it's about. Harry Potter's about a young wizard coming of age and overcoming the Dark Lord. The Avengers are about saving the world, or avenging it when they can't. This is their **standpoint statement,** a self-summary in a few seconds that gets their main idea across. You've probably heard of something similar called an elevator pitch.

What we're doing is similar but puts the focus on you and puts the essence of your spiel in a one-minute monologue. Key components to keep in mind include:

1. **Who's the reader?** *Audience appeal is important.* Who will you be sharing this with? If it's a college admissions counselor, you might emphasize one element over another if you're telling the same to the professor of a class you're sitting in on. Admissions might want to know how you view the school and its impact on your future, while a professor's priorities lie in what you want to achieve in the classroom. Your standpoint statement for each will be different based on readership.

2. **What's it about?** Before you tell me about your "book," think about how you pitch your favorite Netflix shows to friends. Sure, you love it, but what's the general concept, the genre, or what's driving the plot forward? This might be the best story never told if you are poor at explaining it and garnering interest. Remember how many other applicants are in the running, and be sure to find what makes you break away from the pack. And of course,

3. **Why should I keep reading?** I've always heard the first part of this Bobby Womack quote, *"Always leave them wanting more,"* but never the other, *"and you know they'll always call you back."* If your introduction ends on a

cliffhanger, you can bet they'll turn the page, and then if that chapter ends right before some important info is divulged, that's another page turn, and then another, and then you've spent the night in a book. Streaming shows do the same thing, where you likely wouldn't sit down for a four-hour marathon without some preparation but might spend an entire weekend binge-watching a season due to the ease of an ever-unfolding storyline, each episode ending right before an answer.

You need to hook potential schools from the jump and keep them there, especially when there's other content competing for attention. The upside is that once you've sparked interest, that Story Method of remembering is in your favor, linking your standpoint statement to all your other application components. Once you understand yourself, you can understand how to pick a school that's compatible with *your* values.

Think of your favorite stories, movies, books, or Netflix shows. Which kind of protagonist, or main characters, are you most attracted to? And I don't mean physically, but from a narrative standpoint. You may not have even considered it, but we are drawn towards active protagonists over passive ones. The difference? Actives take control, drive the plot forward, and make a difference in their worlds. Passives' paths are completely determined by external factors they take no initiative to control.

In a book or on the silver screen, that's all fine and dandy, but how can this relate to you? My experience with advisers is that it works in theory, but in practice, our unique, individualized situations factor into how abstract advice can be useful in practical application. Let's leave the hypothetical and center on the actual.

What better way to formulate future success than by profiting off prior accomplishments? This is your story, and you should tell it your way.

For the purposes of this book, you will be given stories, from my life and others, the success stories and cautionary tales we've owned up to, and then we'll dive into what we can learn from them. It might not always be obvious, but rest assured, the journey is as essential as the destination.

Still, there is no story without conflict, or a pain point, and that's where strategic storytelling comes into play. And what do you know, the first of five factors for forward momentum is all about personal branding.

And you already know we learn best from stories.

Here is how I re-branded myself as "The Black Kid Who Talks to Klansmen."

1

IT'S NOT THE BRAND THAT'S IMPORTANT, BUT THE BRAND BEHIND YOUR NAME THAT MATTERS

THE KID WHO TALKED
WITH KLANSMEN

———

It was the year 2016, in "post-racial America." Did you know our brains aren't fully formed until we're twenty-five? I was eighteen. Maybe that's why I was mad enough to meet with the kind of person who outright states, "I'd end you without a second on the battlefield."

The battlefield, he claimed, extends from his home to the public schools, from the grocery store to the local movie theater, all the way to the White House. Where there are nonwhites, there are fights, he asserts. Luckily for me, this alt-right sympathizer abided by the rules of engagement I call the law, and the law has a zero-tolerance policy on homicide, regardless of claims concerning white genocide. Hence, he was my favorite Klansman to interview so far.

I had but one question: *Why?*

I asked him, well, let's call him Rob (because that's his name), that one question at the start of our meeting on a brisk September evening in the damp, leaky cellars of what was once called the Edison Hotel in Sunbury, Pennsylvania.

Never heard of it?

That's not on account of it being so easy to look up. It was originally the "City Hotel" when opened in 1871 before being changed to the "Edison Hotel" to better reflect its renown as the birthplace of electricity, thanks to Thomas Edison's discovery there (Klose, Jason). That is, until confusion over its name and eventual addition of a dining section on the ground floor caused the then-management to choose "Hotel Edison Restaurant" to settle the debate.

The irony behind the story is that despite the alterations to name and changing ownership, the general persona remained the same. In fact, that's exactly how Rob described his time with the ever-shifting Keystone State Skinheads. Call them Skinheads or call them "Keystone United"; the name is just the shapeshifting mask, a Rorshach test for the very controversial and expressive face of white pride in central Pennsylvania. You know, the place where I called home for over ten years.

Sometimes violent, other times "just passionate," but always striving to preserve the heritage of their people, Rob found a home and a host of heroes to look up to within their ranks that fascinated him at fifteen years old. With no father in the house and a heart full of hate at the races he blamed for it, he was dedicated from that point forward, ready to "... wage the coming race war and battle the beasts of this world once the nationwide signal was given."

This was powerful stuff, and he meant every word of it.

Black families moved into town as his father left along with the jobs that kept the bills paid and food on the table. Instead of the economy or the hiring managers, he found fault with the different-looking families that began to populate Pennsylvania in the early 2000s, easy-to-spot-in-the-street targets that his newfound friends assured him were the cause of his conflicts.

Rob's rants and rhetoric are unfortunately not uncommon here.

Penns Woods sheltered and shadowed white hoods and was why my adoptive family moved us from Paxinos to Sunbury—that, and finding a burning cross in the neighbors' yard down the road. But what was different about Rob's retelling of the same tired trope, that burden of Black people on the state's resources, and whine of the "wounded warrior white man," was his answer to my original question: *Why?*

"Why what?" he asks.

"Just why."

"Why do I do this? What choice do we have? We're losing our culture, our women, our way of life."

"Why?"

"Black men, Arab men, Hispanic men... all these other races can't stick to their lot. Can't be happy with what they've got, they've got to come and take from us. Our women, our jobs, our nation. And I'm not-"

"Why?"

"Wha-what'd you mean?"

"Why do you think this?"

He snorted then, but gave no response.

Over the course of the next hour and a half, I'd whittled Rob down to childhood traumas and near tears. Not because of me, ironically, but because this may have been the first time someone had continually asked him why. And to think, this interview started off with him refusing to speak to me, with his hand on his sidearm protectively. Though we had a mutual "friend" there, a witness to be sure nothing went awry, Rob never locked eyes with me. I'd ask a question, and he'd turn to our friend as if he were a translator to answer. Still, my questions were answered.

You see, I wouldn't have known this Rob from any other on the street. When I first started working for the hotel/ restaurant that we'll just call "Edison" for clarity's sake, I was fifteen years old. I wasn't old enough to serve the alcohol, but apparently old enough for customers to throw silverware and condiments at. After the third time it happened and the third time we had an angry storm out, my manager asked for a third time, "That guy lose it on you 'cause you're Black?"

And who was I to know for sure. I wasn't one to toss out the race card without regard, but I certainly wasn't about to catch another fork in the forearm. My time working there was short, but sour.

Still, this manager seemed keenly aware of the regulars, and steered me clear of the more difficult-to-please patrons. He'd always considered himself a wine steward, he explained, and people are picky about their wines. Some wore ashy suits, others bore ink-splattered crosses on their neck, just below the collar line. So, after a few years had passed and I found myself in a creative writing class with an assignment prompting us to *seek out and interview individuals from a perspective wildly different from your own,* I knew Edison held the ace that'd get me an A. I trekked back to Sunbury from my college in Selinsgrove (a twenty-minute drive) and point blank asked the old wine steward: Where's the Klansman at, and how do I get ahold of him?

To his credit, he didn't pretend to not know, but assured himself that yes, I really did want to do this and yes, I understood the risk, and no, this was not a death wish. He arranged an audience with Rob, deciding to play mediator and put on the proceedings under his place of business—literally. We weren't about to convene in the amber-lit diners' area above or the modest accommodations even higher in the hotel rooms; no, the mildewy root cellar of the establishment would do just fine, even with the retching pipes.

Rob reared his head into the hold at about five minutes to seven in the evening, just before we were scheduled to meet. First his head, then his gun, and the trembling hand that held it descended into the darkness with us. Heart hammering, eyes dilating, mind racing to the only door out while my feet fixed into place, I feigned a placating smile and threw out a hand to be shaken.

It was not taken.

"That him?" Rob asked, as if I wasn't there, and Steward answered for me.

"Y-Y-Yeah, Rob... just... just... no need for a gun—"

"No need for this." Rob sits in the remaining wooden chair, loudly. "Nothing's going to change anyway. No use talking about it."

And yet, he was here.

He didn't look much different than any other blue-collar you'd meet. An army-green tee folded over a strong frame, one from genetics and hard labor instead of a gym, and jeans faded at the knees only complimented this, with big, bulky black boots to match. Where I expected dark pits were emerald eyes, inflamed with irritation, twisted up and snarled along with a bushy goatee. Oh, and I can't forget the silver glock that thankfully remained in its holster, one meaty hand on its hilt.

You see, what's worrying isn't just what he's saying, or how he's saying it, but the fact that after two decades of what cannot be described as anything less than indoctrination, he appears immovable in his belief. The whites are under attack, and the enemy comes in all shades of brown. His story, the story of so many caught up in the swell of self-hate and hate crimes, shows ignorance, arrogance, and an unwillingness to change. As a transracial adoptee, a Black boy raised by white folks, it's more than a little disheartening.

I asked Rob, "Why do you assume anyone who doesn't look like you is out to get you? Why can't you imagine a world where people with skin like yours can live alongside those with skin like mine? That I'm as human as you?"

"Look, this's been going on longer than we've been alive. Can't be fixed just because we're sittin' here having a talk like it's tea-time."

I smiled. "Why not?"

Education is the ability to listen to almost anything without losing your temper or self-confidence.
ROBERT FROST

MORAL OF THE STORY

Disclaimer: I do *not* advise doing anything dangerous or delusional like that for personal branding purposes.

The point of the story is that I took what was a problem— heck, still a problem in central Pennsylvania— and turned that into my passion: the intersection of education and civil rights. Take that one step further, and you have the kind of story that shows colleges you've been thinking long and hard about what you'll do with your degree and why you need it, and show you're already putting in the work toward attaining those goals. It's the difference between wanting something and working toward it.

Jeff Bezos (I know, I know, just hear me out) revamped the online retail business through personal branding. Now, understand, by the time Bezos launched Amazon as an idea, he'd just left his position as senior vice president for a hedge fund. I let you know that to make sure you understand I'm aware he had money well before becoming the richest man in the world.

He also had his finger on the pulse of propensity, catching on to current trends like the then-recent world wide web, and capitalizing on this investment. And it wasn't perfect. Having the best selection of quality products at the lowest price with the most convenient form of delivery service came with some complications. At the time, his base of operations was out of an abandoned hospital, using copy paper for blinds. Understandably, there was skepticism.

But then it caught on.

When you can find groceries, movies, and this very book all online on Amazon, it definitely says something about your branding.

> *"Your brand is what other people say about you when you're not in the room."*
>
> JEFF BEZOS

In short, personal branding is how the world views you, the people around you, and what you do. Know someone in all the Honors and AP classes with all the answers? They might define their brand as the smart student, a positive net value. Are you or do you know someone who is consistently late for functions? This can have a negative net value, for as Chris Rock states in a 2018 Netflix special, "Late to school, late to work!" This may convey unreliability to prospective employers, all things you don't want them to think.

So how can students improve their personal brand? Remember those examples I gave about highlighting your academic profile?

- Demonstration of leadership potential
- Showing interest in school of choice and career
- Take initiative towards those ends

So, for number one, this is where that old adage of clubs and activities come from. Sure, you have a high GPA, but if you have no experience in anything else, someone more "well-rounded" than you might take the cake on this one. This is only half-true. Leadership experience can be as attainable as leading a school club or getting involved as an upperclassman in a mentorship program for younger students. This one's especially useful, as it hits a few spots to cover. By being a mentor, you show the traits of leadership, and if it's in your field of choice, you also can implement what you want to do and how you hope to accomplish it. The best predictor of future success is past success, so highlighting your expertise in the matter is crucial.

If you can't explain it to a six-year-old, you don't understand it yourself.

ALBERT EINSTEIN

Now, the students you mentor might not be in that exact age range, but the ability to teach is often underappreciated, and anyone who has ever started a new job with a less-than-helpful trainer can attest: teaching is a skill.

Demonstrating interest is as simple as showing the school you are in business. Reaching out to the admissions department over any questions you have about the process (don't worry, I've been on both ends and know I asked more questions than I have ever answered as a professional) and setting up a campus tour are examples of demonstrating interest in a university. It's like stepping on a car salesman's lot; you wouldn't be there if you weren't even slightly interested in buying a car!

And then, there is initiative. Try something that hasn't been done before in your field, or, more manageable, something that's unique to your field or not usually done. A political science hopeful is one thing, but one that has interned with their senator is another. Is that a little out of reach for you? Try creating a website dedicated to covering school or even local politics. For me, I call attention to three core areas that, if you play up, can show your initiative:

1. Informational interviewing is where you reach out to those in your areas of interest and inquire about the field. For this book, I reached out to over thirty individuals even tangentially related to the field of education and in return have just as many offers for employment once graduate school is over. Not only do you learn about the job market you're entering, but you also expand your network to folks who will remember you and your initiative when there's an opening.

Content creation expands on the informational interview by having you create and compile all the information in one place. You won't forget it and it shows you've dedicated time to your passion. If you're a writer, a blog works fine, and if you're skilled in video arts, try your hand at a YouTube channel or a podcast. They're free, easy ways to create sharable content. Speaking of...

2. Sharing is caring, and sharing this with prospectives in your industry or compiling it into a personal website allows others to "visit" you online. We don't always carry our resumes when we meet folks who'd like them, so directing them to an online source of all your prior work is extremely helpful.

When we strive for our goals, we have to be aware, much like Bezos's prior successes, of the unfair advantages we possess going into a situation. We must be cognizant of **situational awareness,** aware of the elements embroiled in everyday interactions. How does your personal branding relate to your personal goals? Identifying your unfair advantages through situational awareness allows you to capitalize on them, turning them into your competitive advantage.

Now what's an unfair advantage?

Unfair advantage refers to the traits and attributes that set us apart from others, the feats that come easier to us than to others. The entire premise is not to get hung up on what others have that you don't, but about identifying and utilizing your own advantage to your favor. For example, I'm no mathematician, but what I lack in natural arithmetic skill really came to bite me in high school. My brother is in a trigonometry class a year or two ahead of schedule. Me? My senior year had me struggling through statistics, the remedial math course they give you just to graduate. I was never great at it, and to this day use apps on my phone to ensure accurate tips when dining out, but found I put myself on a self-defeating path well before I even got into the classroom.

When math was merely mentioned, I'd shut down before the assignments were even handed out. There was a fear of failure that transformed into a heated frustration that led to actual hate towards the subject, as funny as that sounds. To me, math was a constant reminder of how dumb I was. Who likes being reminded of that? I despised the feeling math gave me and in doing so put myself back even *further* by not applying myself in the class that needed the most attention.

It'd take me years to realize I wasn't bad at math, but that it takes me a bit more time to process the mathematical equations than others they come more naturally to. I'd tell myself, *It's not that you're bad at this, just slower than others at it.* Finding shortcuts, spending extra time studying, and, totally serious here, mentally preparing myself for the arduous task of a math problem helped a ton.

Meanwhile, my English and writing classes were some of the most engaging, easy, and energizing I've had. I fell in love with the theater (even dropping football for it) and speech & debate. Yes, I was *that* nerdy. But that nerdiness came with some perks, landing me in the top-forty student speech competitors in the nation, acquiring several awards, and meeting with Pennsylvania's state representatives.

Our school's speech & debate program combined elements of theater, public speaking, and nonprofit work. We met with local leaders in that department to help with their endeavors. So when I found myself debating a Klansman on the ethics of my own existence, it turns out I had the perfect background for it.

But that's not really an *unfair* advantage, is it? Anyone could have applied those communicative skills and attained a similar level of success.

My unfair advantage ties back into *who* was interviewing the Klansman. See, when discussing a point in our lives we've had to resolve a conflict, confront an issue, or go through a particularly grueling experience, we may tend to get uncomfortable, diminish how challenging it was, or altogether not want to divulge further. Some locals in Pennsylvania refer to it, lovingly, as Pennsyltucky, a name derived from the somewhat-backwoods nature of some residents that is often stereotypical of the American Deep South.

Part of that stereotype are the discriminatory views white supremacists hold toward minority populations. So a story of a Black man crossing the color barrier to resolve (or at least try to) conflicts with a Klansman is remarkable. That's not to say a white man doing the same wouldn't have garnered any attention, but a spike of curiosity is attached to it due to the color of my skin. Where I lived in small-town, Sunbury, Pennsylvania, we had a young girl in a neighboring town of Selinsgrove by the name of Hilde Kate Lysiak who took up an interest in investigative journalism—at nine years old, covering local murders.

You can bet Lysiak's actions caught the attention of many. The young girl created her own newspaper, *Orange Street News*, to independently keep the public informed, which led to her own Scholastic book series, an Apple TV+ mystery show, and possibly becoming the world's youngest college commencement speaker at West Virginia University's Reed College of Media. Lysiak took something commonplace, journalism, combined it with her own personal brand as a younger-than-average reporter, and made it something spectacular (Hipes).

Conversing with a Klansman was a piece of cake. Handling the pressure to succeed in an environment I was unfamiliar with was a culture shock. Being on campus means being present, at all times, with so many different walks of life. For some, college is the most diverse place they've ever been. For others, it's the least. For a number of students, going to college was not a question but an expected next step in life after high school, while for others, they were quite literally living the dream they once thought impossible. As a first-generation student, I found it surprising and inspiring how many others were there with me, charting their own path.

We still paled in comparison to the number of legacies— students whose parents had attended the institution prior. That, in and of itself, is not an attribute worth criticism.

What is, though, is when this trait becomes preferential, and less-qualified candidates may get pushed through simply due to their parents' alumni status.

That unfair advantage is why personal branding is vital.

And it turned out I wasn't alone in thinking this.

SPARK OF
SOMETHING NEW

"Well? What'd he have to say to that?"

One of my first-year classmates in my creative writing class asked me this after my retelling of race relations gone wrong. On our first day, we went over the stories of our lives, awkward icebreakers, and a rapid repeating of how and why we chose our undergraduate university. It's day one of the semester, but we've been here about a week. I'll skip over the three-hour welcoming speech for the incoming class but cue you in on the important aspects.

Our introduction to campus was held in an enormous, white-pillared field house, one wide enough to house a mile-long indoor track beside its indoor pool and an entire weightlifting facility. It was state of the art, that's to be sure, a community gathering point for the small woodland town it resided in. When there wasn't a few hundred incoming first-years, city citizens could be found taking advantage of all the indoor amenities, or a few feet outside running along the outdoor track that outlined the football field.

Lucky for me, my first-year residence hall, the smallest of the bunch, directly overlooked the field house and the football field right next to it, a perfect viewing spot for football games and a quick two-minute stroll from the introductory ceremony our college president called us for. It might've been a few hours long in procedure, and I know a few of us fell asleep in our chairs, but I was only a minute away from my new home away from home.

In fact, the small, quaint campus nestled itself under an emerald canopy of trees granting the red-bricked buildings a cool shade beneath their leaves. The college was created along a steady incline of a hill, perfect for the early-morning runner I was. Ten minutes can get you from one end of campus to the other—six if you're in decent shape and jog. Even better, you rarely had to do that, not with residence halls next to academic halls next to cafeterias at the upper end of the hill. Only the gymnasium had me at the other end, and hey, I could use the walk back up the hill to grab some grub.

Another aspect of campus life for us was the outdoor classes, where the actual school site expanded beyond our walled enclosures into greener pastures. Down the hill, into town, and down by the riverside, we held a brainstorming session for our writing class. The Susquehanna River crested on muddy shores below us, lapping at our constructed classroom as newfound friends swapped stories—and suspicion.

"You didn't *really* meet like, a *real* Klansman, though, right?" someone asked.

"It's like, a metaphor, you know?" said another. "Just a real bad guy's all. Not to take away from your story or nothin', but no way you, I mean, *you,* Noah the Fenstermacher, faced down one of those, those... cultists... and lived to tell the tale!"

"What can I say; it's all true," I said, but even then, some were unconvinced.

"And what if I still don't believe you?"

I quickly grasped at the air as if to catch a fly.

"Sorry," I told him. "There goes the last care I had." Of course, I didn't say *care*; it was another four-letter word I'd just run out of. But I think you get the point, and the class did too, howling away on that beautiful day by the water.

"Fresh out? Damn," a voice called out from down on the banks. "And here I was hoping to hear more."

Enter Sterling, the upperclassman with a name as bright as his future.

Honestly, I'd never met the guy before, but everyone knew him; how could you not? He was on every pamphlet and mailing package I got from the university, headlined all the main orientation events for us first-years, and was *the* tour guide for campus. Sure, there were others, and I'm sure they did just as well giving tours, but Sterling? He gave *experiences*, the kinds of tours the professors and college presidents would stop and interact with—the kind that lent you the storytelling rights just for having been on the tour with him. He gave the VIP tours to visiting professionals because he was the president's favorite pupil.

See, Sterling stuck out at 6'4", dark skinned, and big voiced among his usual crew: a Greek life organization (a fraternity, they called it?) of mostly white men that he stood apart from. Those guys were always seen around the president at campus events, so I figured Sterling was just always at the heart of the action. The fact that he was down here, away from his regulars, away from the sights and sounds, I won't lie, was nerve-wracking. It was like the star of the show came out into the crowd, and there I was caught whispering to a neighbor.

"Well, unfortunately, that's... that's the end of the story." I told him.

"Hey, hey, I didn't come down to ruin the fun. I's actually lookin' for ya."

And now, the audience member was invited onstage.

"Good thing we've just finished up!" I said while hurriedly packing my things.

Class was basically over anyway, or at least, it was now with no professor for this "self-guided" portion and with Sterling leading me off back toward campus. He walked with the inclination I was to follow, and I quickly did while the rest of the class went about their parting pleasantries.

"Was there something you wanted to talk with me about?" I asked with hesitation.

"Yeah, man. So, like, this story you've been telling people..."

Uh-oh.

"...it's incredible. I mean, totally dangerous, stupid, unnecessarily provocative, but legit. Yeah, real legit, I'll give ya that. Admissions department's lookin' for someone like that, someone to liven things up for newcomers comin' in for a campus visit. World's wisin' up on what Black and Brown kids can bring to the table, mean's they gotta reflect the kinda students they wanna see. Needs more Black is what I'm sayin'. Needs smart, funny, witty, sexy, whatever, but Black excellence. And hey, that just might be you."

He gave a glamorous outlook, gassing me up with every compliment given. Being a tour guide is fun, exciting, and people focused. The only campus job I could find when I first got here was in the football locker room washing the used gear and jock straps of the players. I mean, we had a washer, but still. I was so thrilled by the first part of the question I almost missed the follow up.

"So, whattya say?"

"Wha-... y-yeah... yeah! I'd love to, man. Thanks for asking! Can't wait to get in there and get started. In fact, when's my first day? I can start tomorrow if you need—"

"Woah, woah, woah. Slow your roll, brother." He said with a hearty laugh, that trademark bellow that echoed across the halls. "I'll let 'em know later today you're psyched... *super* psyched for the opportunity. Might take a few days, but we'll get you all squared away. If ya have time, though, might wanna stop by the House on the Hill."

"The what now?"

"House on a Hill, man! C'mon, that's where all of us get together. You don't gotta answer right now, but if you're lookin' to join up with a fraternity... you should totally join up with—"

For the sake of protecting identity, I won't use their name here, if only for their role in the story later. In place of their official name, I'll refer to them by the way it was described to me.

"Fraternal Order?" I remember being confused. "Sounds kinda... cult-y to me, no offense. Aren't you guys, like, 'party people?'" I swear to God, I even did the air quotes, but, luckily, Sterling wasn't offended.

"I get it, we get a bad rap in the media, but you and I know better than most that what they say about us in the news isn't always true, ya feel?"

And how could I say no to that?

"Yeah, yeah," I answered. "I'll come visit you up there. Last house on the hill—"

"*Only* house on the hill, so that should be easy. Right across from the campus church and the student resource center. Don't worry, man, you'll figure it all out in time. I got big hopes for ya," now clapping me on the back. "It's a long four years. Hey, could be me, I only learned a lot of this on my own after two years here, so count yourself lucky! You're at one of the best schools in the state with one of the best stories around! We'll teach all ya need to know, and before long you'll be teaching your own underclassmen."

"And everything the light touches will be our kingdom?" And on this, I got a genuine smile, his eyes sparked open and that telltale yell of joy leapt to life.

"YO! You're funny, too? I'm tellin' ya man, big things!"

He had no idea how much that meant to me.

My parents always referred to opportunities not like windows or doors but like sparks, these short bursts of energy and light that, if left unfettered, can blink out without a trace. Maybe it's because we loved camping, and you can't have a camp without a campfire. The spark of something new means somehow two or more things came together in just the right way as to create the fire, and if you had this burning passion for it you'd best get to tending that fire. And like a flame, it wasn't something quick and done with, but something that took time and careful maintenance; so too will building your personal brand as you also take advantage of these small sparks of something new.

But even little fires can burn a big forest, and, as we'd find out, even one student can have an impact on many.

LEAVING THE NEST

"I do have a few questions first," I said to Sterling. "How'd you become... you? I mean, have all these opportunities, the fraternity, the president? Like, you're everywhere, man."

"Appreciate it, thank ya, thank ya, but, ah, didn't have much of a choice. I'm first-gen, first in the family to get to college so if I didn't make opportunities... well, they didn't come a-knockin' at my door so to speak."

"You're first-gen, too? So am I!"

"Seriously?"

"Yes! Oh my god, this is great! I thought I was the only one, I mean, I've been the only one for so long."

"Guessin' college isn't a natural next step back where you're from?"

"You mean across the river? Not for everyone, no."

"Oh, dang, you're right over there, huh? Sunbury, then. Not a lot of Black folks from what I've seen."

You're telling me. I'd never been ashamed of who I was; the innocence of children has yet to be tainted by the prejudices of adults. I remember one kid specifically who just assumed I was "Brown"—that we were all kids, one just a darker shade than the others. Of course, we all have to grow up someday.

"You're looking at them," I said. "I'm one of, like, five. I was adopted into a white family so my brother and I, we're the only two Black boys—"

"In a white world." He whistled. "Damn. How's that even go? Like, how'd ya stay in touch with your culture being out here in the boonies?"

"Honestly, I... I never really had Black culture. My parents did what they could but I was adopted pretty young."

"Sheesh. Their world is all you know? When were you adopted again?"

"1998, right outta Philly. When I say young, I mean a few days old kind of young." As I said this, he beamed in reply.

"Philadelphia, yo, that's where my folks are from!"

"Yep, right outta the hospital over by—" And I told him where.

And he paused.

"Huh. 1998, that hospital... I know this is, like, really weird and all, but do you remember what adoption agency you had?"

I told him, and he paused again.

"It's like... I had a baby brother, just born, never met him, but they sent him up for adoption with that agency and like..."

"Unless your mom's name is K----- S-----, I hate to break it to ya, but it's not a match." I told him. "Just looked up my ancestry on this site and I have all the info down for my bio folks."

It was scribbled on a crumpled note, a stash of secrets scrounged away in my class materials, just waiting to be unraveled and followed up on. Truth be told, I was nervous; big revelations tend to do that to you. I could sense Sterling wanting to press me, but I appreciated him backing off at seeing my unease talking about it. A small gesture goes a long way.

"Hey, if we're not brothers by blood, we'll be 'em by bond, yeah? I'm real happy for ya, though. Seriously, you've got a knack for some good stories, you know that? Guess you've got time to tell *that* story whenever you're good and ready."

"And I am not in the slightest," I replied. "All their info's sitting in a drawer in my room, just waiting for the right time, I guess."

"Ah, well, from what I've found, man, there's rarely a 'right time' for anything, ya just make time for what's right." This he said while draping an arm over my shoulder and leading us both back toward campus grounds.

Not everyone gets a pseudo-big brother the moment they step on campus. I was lucky and grateful to have the advice and mentorship. We talked as we walked, and I'll share the ten items we discussed that helped solidify my stellar first year.

10 THINGS YOU NEED TO SUCCEED

1. **Engage with an extracurricular that connects to your career,** so you will have some transferable experiences you can highlight in interviews and in the job you will attain. Have fun, and if the fun can factor into your post-graduate life, all the better!
2. **Learn how to study,** since, if you're a little like me, you may not have done a whole lot of that in high school. Or, maybe you *thought* you did. To me, studying was just reading and then rereading the material, often glancing at it throughout the weeks leading up to a test and then, sad to admit, cramming at the last minute. I didn't even know there were official ways to study! Luckily, you have three prominent techniques at your disposal.

a. SQ3R: **S**urvey by skimming through chapters, headings, and other items that jump out at you before asking **q**uestions around each chapter's central premise. Then, **r**ead the content in full and search for the answers to the questions you posited before **r**eciting, or, putting the content in your own words. Finally, **r**eview to ensure you have a comprehensive understanding of the text.

b. Spaced practice, as the name implies, is the exact opposite of the cram-the-night-before that I used to do. Breaking down the text into an hour, or even a half hour a day, leading up to the event ensures your brain won't go into overdrive to recall vast amounts of information from only a few hours before the test.

c. The last studying strategy is called the Feynman technique, and while you might not know the name, you're familiar with the concept. After you've spaced out your studying habits and utilized SQ3R to effectively gather data, you'll need a method to demonstrate your mastery of the materials. Simply put, Feynman shows you've learned something by teaching or explaining it to others. If you can communicate the concept to someone else, then you fully understand it yourself.

3. **Buy your books online and ahead of time** to take advantage of the lowered prices for renting them (either through your campus bookstore or Amazon, whichever's cheaper).

4. **Create a class schedule** to help plan out your semesters. If you're not a fan of early-morning seminars at 8:00 a.m., have a few schedules where afternoon or evening times are preferred. You might not always get your first pick, so being flexible is key.

5. **It's a dorm, not a hotel,** so don't emphasize your experience with the amenities when you're here for the academics. Yes, the room may not be as spacious as what you've seen in movies, but it gets the job done. That's not to say you should accept poor conditions—far from it—but remember why you're here and don't get caught up on the little details.

6. **Don't play the comparison game** as there are no winners. We all start at different checkpoints, some first-generation students who have no frame of reference for all things academic, and some third-generation legacies who've practically grown up near campus. Some are naturally more athletic or academic, and you should not waste time comparing yourself to their journeys when you should be focusing on yours. Otherwise, you'll spend your time looking at everyone else's progressing stories and not advancing your own.

7. **Get good grades from the get-go,** as it is difficult to recover from a low GPA at the start of your first year... and yes, I would know. I had a scholarship nearly revoked for how low mine became during my transition to college classes, and though I brought it back up, it was a wake-up call I won't forget.

8. **Keep connections and create new ones.** Don't forget mom and pop back home or childhood friends, but don't be afraid to make new acquaintances. Staying shut up in your room leaves you missing out on amazing opportunities, and as we'll get into later, you have no idea where they'll go!

9. **Your roommate may not be your best friend.** As Sterling pointed out, this one's more about managing expectations. The first people you meet might not be your ride-or-dies

for those four years, and that's perfectly fine. My room-mate, Adrien, a red-haired, gun-loving smartest fool I've ever met, turned out to be one of mine, but if they're not, don't feel like you've failed or are missing out on some aspect of college.

10. **College may not be all it's cracked up to be.**

"Woah, woah, woah." I jumped back in. "What's that last one mean? You're *the* tour guide around here, shouldn't you be tellin' everybody and their mother, literally, that we're just the best thing since shows starting streaming?"

"I'm just saying ya might not love every second of it. I mean, I do, but I'm not everyone," he said with a wink. "Tryin' to manage expectations here. Everyone thinks it's like the movies and, surprise, it's not. So some hate it because it's not what they expected. I'd rather have 'em tiptoe into two feet of water rather than diving in headfirst."

"No diving, then," I said.

"No diving indeed," he agreed. "Oh. And you shouldn't ask or give free advice."

"Did you *not* just do that?"

"Do as I say, not as I do, young Padawan. What I'm saying is, don't just toss out blanket advice and don't just go around popping questions and then leaving. Like, if you're wanting advice, do your homework first. See what sites are out there and then follow up with some people. Shows you actually care about what you're talking about. That whole feed a man, teach a man difference. Flip side of the coin, don't offer advice ya can't use. I'm so sick of hearing pseudo-philosophy like, 'It is what it is' and 'Some things never change.' Yeah, and some things do; you've learned nothing!"

So, for our first-generation students and students of color out there, here's some resources you can access:

1. This helpful site, TheCollegeBoard.org, is perfect for Free Application for Federal Student Aid (FASFA) questions.
2. First in the Family, which even has summer programs specifically for low-income minority students.
3. Affordable Colleges Online, which even possesses a "First-Generation College Student Guide" to help you walk through the process and transition to campus.

"Well don't you just have it all together. The man with a plan and a way to advance," I said, and he shrugged in response.

"Hey, I had to learn the hard way. Shouldn't have had to, but if I can help someone else, it was all worth it, you know?" he said.

He had no idea how much that meant to me.

I still remember the blur that was my graduation, a rush of endorphins and ceremony and parents crying for their kids' big moment—the hurry up and wait of it all, that moment you take the paper freeing you from life's free trial and sending you straight into a pay-to-play subscription. Tears flowed freely around, a few caps were thrown and caught, and people scurried away into minivans as everyone headed off to parties celebrating their achievement.

But there was one parent crying for a different reason.

After accepting my diploma, I went and visited the mother of my childhood best friend, Kurtis. See, Kurtis caught leukemia a few years back, and didn't make it to graduation. I remember him as happy as any of us, bright eyed and full of laughter. I remember as those eyes darkened, his skin slid into shades of sickly yellow, and his laughs were replaced by coughs. After a few months, a lot of other kids got scared, leaving him and I alone to work together. A few more, and even I got scared, helping this kid a few days older than me up two flights of stairs, him sweating and straining all the way. These were the worries of someone with an aging parent, not a sick second grader. I remember the day he didn't come in to school—the day we were told he'd gone to the hospital.

The day they told us yesterday was his last day in school. I remember a child's funeral giving death such a young face.

After senior graduation, I presented his mother with a gift our class made, a memorial, a remembrance of life with the class he would've graduated with and can still feel the embrace she gave me I felt had been stolen from him.

"It's so great to see you grown up," she told me, and I wish she could say it to her own son.

Kurtis passed away years ago in elementary school, though every year our family hangs an ornament in his memory on the Christmas tree. It still stung, year after year, this one especially so as it would be the last with a yearbook to remember him by. This was where all of us, all us spunky upstarts, were supposed to be the big thinkers and get out of our old central Pennsylvanian town to take on the world. Now we're one short.

I wonder what the world would have been like if he was still with us. It's not survivor's guilt I have; you can't feel self-reproach for a sickness you have no sense over. But I do feel like doing *something* with the life I have that others have not been fortunate enough to keep.

This I reflected on while bathing in the amber sun, a bright ambiance bouncing off the blades of grass, freshly cut, from our fenced-off forever home. It was a perfect fit for our family of five. I remember the surprise, not well kept, of a graduation party in our backyard. My parents were there, two redheads taking shelter under a picnic canopy, and their fiery-haired youngest son right beside them. That's Luke. The middle child, Jonah, is off to the side, engrossed in a game on his phone. Our maternal grandparents are here as well, and macaroni and still-steaming cheese with bacon in a dish they walk up with together.

I am blessed I was adopted into such a loving family. We both are, Jonah and I, two Black children four years apart in this light-toned family, their biological son Luke four years *his* junior. Noah, Jonah, and Luke—can you tell we went to church on Sundays? We went and we prayed and we thanked for all that we had, all the opportunities that had graced us by. I was going to be the first in the family to attend college, something my grandfather couldn't be prouder of.

"My grandson, a college graduate! I'm surprised but I know I shouldn't be. You've always had what it takes to get out there, now everyone else is gonna see what I see every day." He jumped from his chair and saluted me, so sudden and surprising we all nearly jumped.

"Hey, Pap? What are you—" I asked.

"I'm saluting my grandson," he said, returning to rest and extending his hand. "And I'm shaking the hand of the next great man."

Pap, a retired command sergeant major of the Pennsylvania National Guard, was a big believer in the impact even one great man (though I'm sure he'd agree it can be one great person) can have on history—how universal change starts with you, just one person with passion and a plan to pursue it. I'd always heard him reference past presidents, military leaders, and maybe his favorite football player, but now he was speaking about me.

"I...I dunno, Pap. That's some high praise I don't know if I can live up to."

He smiled.

"I do."

DECIDE YOUR CIRCLES OF TRUST

In short, we can't do this alone.

Like we said before, is anyone truly self-made? I'd venture to think not, and to help improve your personal brand, you'd best believe our self-image is at least in part determined by those around us. So surround yourself with positive, supportive figures that also want to help you like Sterling, my Pap, and other loved ones in your life. There are three primary supporters you might find helping you along:

- Accountability partners: peers and near-peers like Sterling; folks who are going through or have very recently gone through what you are now and can directly work with you to accomplish goals. They're like having the best friend that makes sure you're on top of your stuff, and you in turn watch out for them as well. As your fellow foxhole buddy, you keep an eye out for their best interests, as Sterling did for me with the open admissions office position. Not to be confused with...

- Campus champions: Dr. Yolanda E. Norman is the founder & CEO of FirstGenConsulting, L.L.C. and Associate Vice President of Student Development for

Concordia University Texas. She is a nationally known speaker and adviser on all things concerning first-generation college students and taught me all about the concept of "campus champions" when we interviewed.

Campus champions are mentors, figures at college that students can trust and have pertinent knowledge on what it means to be a college student navigating these spaces... They are comfortable, competent, and caring for their advisees.

DR. YOLANDA NORMAN

Having even one person in your corner can make all the difference, and these campus champions can easily substitute for what I describe as living "success stories" of folks who've made it and can now guide others on similar paths. When building your personal brand on campus, all aspects of it will come into question, including race, gender, political beliefs, and religious affiliations. Dr. Michael A. Baston, the president of Rockland Community College, spoke on the impact of

• Affinity groups

To my students of color... You need to get student memberships in affinity groups where opportunities can happen for you if your college does not have these readily set... If you want to be an accountant, you want to get involved with the NABA (National Association of Black Accountants).

DR. MICHAEL A. BASTON

Affinity groups are everything. For some, college is their first time away from home, and having a little culture coming with them might make all the difference. Whether it be your socioeconomic status, your racial identity, or first-generation student status, these aspects can be shared with others and through that connection can be mutual understanding and growth.

"And you think, what, *anyone* can just change their public image? Turn that franchise around? For some of us here, it's just not possible."

This came from Sterling at our lunch table, with all the Black kids sitting together in the crowded cafeteria. He's introduced me to his friends, and small talk evolving into heated debate. We'd gone from how the reality TV star-turned-presidential candidate couldn't *possibly* win to more personal matters. That's where our faction fractured into fighting, so to speak.

"Right?" shouted another student from across the table.

"Sure, it's harder for some people," I admitted. "But just giving up—"

"Never said that," Sterling corrects.

"Right. I know. But if we're saying it's impossible for some people—"

"Didn't say that either."

"Listen, alright! I know, I know. *You're* not saying anything, but what *I'm* saying is, whether it's easier or harder, we've all gotta compete for what we want in life. Yeah, it's easier for some and harder for others, but, like... we've all got hardships you know?"

Everyone disliked that, as a collective eyeroll spread across the room.

"Lemme guess," Sterling starts. "You're gonna say we should all 'pull ourselves up by our bootstraps.'"

"Well... not exactly."

"You've gotta be kidding me."

"No, no, let me finish," I said. "I mean, I hate being told to pull myself up by my bootstraps. It's like, what about the folks who don't have bootstraps? What then?"

"Exactly. See, guys, he isn't completely hopeless."

"But," I continued, "we can't change the system overnight. We can work on correcting it, but what about right here and now? What if we had the means by which to 'pull ourselves up' in the meantime, just laying around the house? Metaphorically, I mean. Like, some symbolic strings, ribbons, or twine. What if we already had what it took to succeed, and it's how we measure success that needs changing?"

Sterling paused mid-bite.

"You had my interest, kid. Now? You've got my attention." And an armistice in arguing seemed to signify agreeance.

"So, then... what's the biggest problem facing underprivileged kids?" I started. "Our lack of access to these opportunities that someone else is basically born into. Their resumes and all are always more full and focused because they could fly across the world to volunteer or, you know, their dad knew so-and-so's dad who worked in the senator's office. What I'm suggesting is we turn those words in our favor. **Bootstrapping** could work for us, and we could use the skills and experiences we already have. Listen, my parents... we didn't have much, Sterling."

"You mentioned," Sterling said.

"My dad was a cement truck driver, took the job because he was getting too old to climb the telephone poles anymore. And my mom? She went from cafeteria worker to custodian because, turns out, they make a little more. And the first thing she asked me before taking the job? If I'd be embarrassed to see her during the day."

An uncomfortable hush fell over the table.

"And you know what? I told her, 'To hell with them. A job's a job and anyone who thinks otherwise is the ass if you ask me,'" which got a few thumps from the others, and a sympathetic understanding all around.

"But you know what? That's how my mom remembers it. Me? I just remember a second of it. That one *second* that I hesitated to answer. I said what I meant and meant what I said, but for a fraction of an instant, I hesitated... I'm not ever gonna forget that."

"Jesus, man, I'm... I'm sorry." Sterling said.

"But that's the thing! I wasn't raised with some of the advantages of others, yeah, but I was working since I was fifteen to help the family. I took a server job, and tutored other kids, and helped the local nonprofits... all that boils down to **transferable skills.** I didn't know that until late in the game, but we've got just as much to offer as these rich kids! I think... I think if we knew how to use them... or at least how to get that across on a resume or in an interview... maybe we could turn things around, you know?"

"That doesn't solve the systemic issue."

"No, it doesn't." I admitted. "But we both know that systemic change is slow—multigenerational. We might be grandparents ourselves before we see any significant impact, and all the while, how many hundreds of thousands of applicants won't even *try* because they don't know how, or get passed over because they didn't know how to use what they already had? What I'm suggesting is only a start, yeah, but we need that spark to get things rolling, you know?"

Although Sterling fell silent, the table returned to bickering among themselves and split down the middle on opinion. He stared into an abyss for seconds that felt endless before saying:

"Yeah, man... maybe we do need someone like you after all."

"Hey! Hey, Noah! Over here."

A high, clear voice called out from across the hall. I saw my new roommate, Adrien, with his fiery tips peeking out over a forest of unfamiliar faces. He sat at round table with Lyss, this pretty pixie gal who serves as our resident assistant, and an Asian American woman I hadn't met, who's confident and waving me over.

I let my table know I'm heading out and go over to make some lifelong friends, pulling up a chair and joining the chat.

"Thanks for comin' over! I just kinda sorta totally eavesdropped on your convo when I passed by and wanted to say I *completely* agree with what you're saying."

"Uh, thanks," I said. "Sorry, I'm Noah. Adrien's my roommate. And you are?"

"Annalise," she said with an outstretched hand. "Very nice to meet you. Adrien's said a lot about you. Apparently we're the two mixed-ish kids here."

"Mixed-ish?" I asked.

"Yeah, mixed-ish. I know you're not, like, literally mixed like me, but he was telling me you've basically got a foot in both worlds. That's like, really cool, honestly." She jerked her head back toward my other table. "Sorry that can be difficult sometimes."

It was.

"It's not," I said. "You get used to it is all. I mean, that's my life, been living it eighteen years so can't say I'm not used to it, right?"

She thought for a moment. "So you're either big fish in a little pond or little fish in a big one?"

"What's that now?"

"Studies show how students see themselves, their **academic self concept,** is directly related to their placements in higher- or lower-achieving schools and programs. Social comparison is all. Quote on quote, big fish in a little pond, or higher-achieving students in lower- or average-achieving programs have a more positive self-concept." She leaned forward. "And it's been shown self-concept is a better predictor of future performance than grades, scores, socioeconomic status, you name it. How someone views themselves... *that's* what makes all the difference."

She leaned back into her chair and said, "And college? We're, like, all the big fish from our little ponds all dumped into one big one. These first few weeks, everybody's gonna be fighting to be the biggest fish in this big pond, but you? Seems like you've already got a good head on your shoulders. A pretty positive self-concept."

"I... thank you, I think?" I said.

"What I'm saying is, you've already got what it takes to succeed out here. I dunno, I know what it's like to have opinions go against the grain of what it means to be Asian or a woman or whatever." Glancing at Sterling holding court a few feet away, she said, "I'd hate for that to get stomped out of you. Long story short, do you and forget everybody else."

What a woman.

When it came to circles of trust, she, Adrien, and Lyss joined Sterling at the center, and for his part, Sterling got me that interview... I just didn't realize all that came with it.

YOUR POSITIONALITY IN INTERSECTIONALITY

———

I waited outside two alabaster pillars; the front of the building could've been a replica of the Parthenon in Greece, as the white stood apart from the green grass that surrounded it and the fifty or so other buildings, all smaller and bricked in reds and browns. I did my research: the building's architect had specifically designed it as the only white-laden structure in sight as a beacon; anyone searching for the college would inevitably have to find its admissions department, and here it would be, the only one of its shade. I was out on its polished deck, stealing glances inside the glass-walled conference room where a gathered meeting took place, when an intensely-blue-eyed receptionist called me in.

"Noah! Thank you so much for coming; I'm the visit coordinator."

I only bring this up because from this memory, that's one of the only shining (pun unintended) details I can recall. I focused on her eyes to keep from looking all around, with my hands on my knees to keep them from shaking, and a forced smile to keep the fear down. In short, I did everything I'd advise you *not* to do. She asked the typical questions one would expect from an interview, but let me tell you, it's much different when you're sitting in that chair, fearing every word can sink your chances, and so I tried to say as few as possible.

"So, tell me about yourself, Noah!"

"What are your greatest strengths?"

"What are your greatest weaknesses?"

"How did you first hear about this position?"

Finally, one I could answer: "Actually, my friend Sterling brought up the idea—"

"*Sterling?*" I remember her eyes lit up even more than they'd been already, and she was now on the edge of her seat. "Oh my god, we absolutely *love* Sterling here. Did you know he works here? Come to think of it... yes, yes he *did* mention you! We've already hired a lot of your brothers from the Fraternal Order. I'm sure you'll make a fine addition to the team."

I also remember telling her only second-semester first-years could be accepted into the Order, how she waved a hand and said how silly she was, and how much smoother the interview went from there. I didn't know if it was her, me, or that somehow the goodwill bestowed upon the Fraternal Order's members was now prematurely bestowed on me, but I felt much more rejuvenated after it was over, and less surprised than I should have been when I received word I got the position. I'd be a student ambassador, the fancy title they gave us even though I was just as happy being a tour guide.

"What'd I tell ya?" Sterling said as we celebrated that night. "You. Were. Worried! And ya had nothing to worry about. All that whimpering and whining and hootin' and hollerin for nothin'!"

"Maybe so. Can't help but think you played a pretty big part in getting this passed through. Second your name came up, I don't know, things just started going a lot smoother in there. Felt like a lot of weight got taken off my shoulders."

"'Least I could do, brah. We need all the help we can get out here."

"I guess so."

"You... you parents really never gave you 'the talk,' did they?"

"...the birds and the bees...?"

"No! No, like, 'the talk.' About the way the world is."

"My family told me about racism, yes," I said. "I'm Black. They're white. Some people might have a problem with that. 'Those that mind don't matter and those that matter don't mind,' yadda yadda. But I'm guessing you're about to go into a whole lot more detail."

"Oh, I most certainly am."

To understand it, though, you've got to have a grasp on **intersectionality** and your **positionality** in it.

Intersectionality refers to the crossing of identity markers and their inherent values within a theoretical framework. Picture a series of Venn diagram circles, with the intersecting sections labeled *White, Black, Man, Woman, Straight, LGBTQ+, First-Generation, Legacy Admit, Higher Income,* and *Lower Income.* You may be in some but not all, and that can increase or decrease the probability of the privilege you may have had afforded to you and the discrimination you may face in higher education and beyond.

For example, a *poor, Black woman* would fall under three separate groups that all faced institutional pressures requiring the Civil Rights Acts to even attend certain higher education institutions. So someone belonging to the *rich, white man* sector has had more **access** to college and, through their higher-earning (family) status, more **resources** from which to draw from to achieve those goals.

This is not to race-bait or point fingers, but to draw a comprehensive map of privilege and how it can impact your chances realistically. Simply belonging to one or all of the groups also doesn't guarantee a free ride, as a rich white man would still need to have the adequate grades to even be considered by colleges.

You can't deregulate hate, but you can provide access and resources to minoritized groups most impacted by it.

To be honest, I hate that the conversation has to be had. Everyone should be treated with the same general respect, regardless of color or culture. I'm discussing here how social factors determine **access** and **resources** to hopefully minimize any negative connotations. I'll refer to privileged groups as **in-group** and underprivileged minorities as **out-group.** Concerning the above Civil Rights example, white students would be the in-group, as black students had to have legal intervention to even attend, making them the out-group due to a lack of privilege.

As a *first-generation, Black* college student from a *lower-income family,* I didn't have a whole lot afforded to me, right? I didn't have the access (literally) to college or even a frame of reference for what is expected of me at college since I'd be in the first in the family to go. In addition, most schools, from my limited perspective at the time, were too expensive for me to go to and so I greatly narrowed my search to what I could afford.

And let's be honest: what eighteen-year-old without a smorgasbord of scholarships is going to pay for that at the point of graduation? No, this would be a family decision—a loan taken out that I'd pay later, and the household working up some cash to pay for books in the meantime.

I could have easily spun the story to one of how I would *need* extra assistance due to my disadvantages, and that is true, but I chose to utilize my unfair advantages so my challenges would make me a change agent for the university. I cited those three Es, too:

- My **experiences** with the National Speech & Debate Association and the National Forensic League helped refine my public speaking, and I used it when interviewing some potentially dangerous individuals.

- My **extracurriculars** that included theater, public speaking, nonprofit work, and speech writing put me in connection with US representatives and local officials.

- My **entrance essay** brought it all together as I explained how my extracurriculars lead to my unique experiences, which allowed me to demonstrate my leadership potential as captain of the award-winning debate team, show interest by reaching out to the school specifically (linking my career aspirations to the specific courses you could take at the university to show more than a surface-level interest), and, of course, my race-relations work to highlight the initiative taken to make the world a better place.

I am *not* saying you go out there and do something dangerous—absolutely not. I'm implying that with great risk comes great reward. Don't get yourself hurt out there, but do make a difference in your field by thinking outside the box to demonstrate for college admissions professionals that not only do *you* take risks, but that they can take the risk on you. The central conceit here is to ensure the message they get, loud and clear, is:

I will succeed because I am determined to, and I want to do it with you.

You've led a club, started another, have useful experience, have fine-tuned that winning personality so no one could reject you, right? Now answer what makes you different from all the other candidates. If you want to be the next Mark Zuckerberg tech titan, did you create a high-tech solution to one of your school's problems? Maybe you want to be an educator, so did you create unique video content breaking down harder lessons for anyone to learn from?

I'm purposefully going over examples that you can do 'on a budget,' so anyone with the willpower and a Wi-Fi connection can accomplish them! No international volunteer trips or big city-based internships, though they are incredible opportunities. I can't recall just how many New York City-based internships I had to miss out on due to the cost of just *getting* there, let alone affording the cost of staying there for a summer.

Once you've identified your unfair advantage, determined your positionality, and have your competitive edge, you're well on your way to developing your winning personality and achieving the academic goals you set out for, as it's not about attending the "cream of the crop" college, but about obtaining the opportunities in your chosen career path. It's not where you go to get your degree, but what you do with it that's important—not the brand name of the university, but the brand behind your name that matters.

"Right, so, like, we're saying the same thing," I said as Sterling and I finished our conversation. "Everyone has hardships, life is unfair, and we have to control what we can control. Use what we've got to stand out in a crowd."

"Yeah, the point's there, you just need a little... refining. C'mon. I think you just need a little hands-on experience to see what I'm saying."

LEARNED HELPLESSNESS

The parable of the pedestrian is pretty simple in concept. The story goes that a pedestrian crosses the street at the crosswalk when they are struck by a car. In this idealized setting, the pedestrian was walking with the light and the driver ran a red light, putting the blame squarely on the oncoming traffic. The driver is then liable to help return the injured pedestrian to a state of relative health through payment for medical care. Sounds simple enough, right?

Now consider that the damage from the incident is major, requiring not only extensive surgery, but a long road to recovery through physical rehab. As someone who's torn their left pectoral completely off the bone (long story) in a weightlifting accident, I can attest the pathway to peace of mind and body is paved with pitfalls (sometimes literally) and setbacks through re-injuring yourself if you're not careful (longer story).

But if the pedestrian refuses to admit themselves for the necessary rehabilitation, where does the fault fall now? It's not the pedestrian's fault they were struck—that's on the driver—but if the driver has since paid his debt and the walker refuses to take the necessary steps to recover, does the onus now fall on them? For the longest time, this was how I perceived racial relations to be: a delicate balance of responsibility, apology, and reciprocity that had no clear beginning or end.

Affirmative action, then, is an act of assistance, a helping hand that guides underprivileged students through those golden gates into the haven of haves at higher education. Colleges aren't handing out aced exams or signed diplomas upon entry, are they? So, once in, the minority students still have to earn the grades they receive, so this isn't a handout by any means.

That's how I saw it, and referenced it, as Sterling walked me into our campus's Black student union, a loose collective of social activists for racial justice I'd never heard of before. Then again, had I been looking? We went through the main student services building back into a long room with a table as lengthy as the space it occupied, enough for thirty or so people to line either side of it and stare upward at Sterling and I at the head of it.

Tensions were high as my first year on campus was also an election year; the appointing of our forty-fifth president was met with much fanfare. The reality star-turned-national leader didn't feel like reality to some, including everyone in that room. Talk of how *a racist president will push racist policies for the next four years* dominated the conversation.

Maybe Sterling picked the wrong night to have me over.

We're polar opposites, as always. Sterling's eyes narrowed and he was heated as ever. My pupils dilated, while I tried (and failed) to calm the room back down.

"Oh, hell no!"

"He didn't! He did *not* just say it's *our* fault!"

"Who the hell is he, anyway?"

"He's one of *us!*" Sterling snarled at the assembled. "He's a brother, and he's here to learn from us about *us.* Last thing we wanna do is turn him away so kindly *shut up!*"

I guess he had some sway built in over the last few years because that worked. Cowed and more than a little confused, an awkward silence fell over the room that just had to be broken.

"Listen, I'm... I'm Noah. I'm a first year from Sunbury—yeah, right across the bridge there—and I'm trying to learn more about... me. I'm adopted into a white family and, don't get me wrong, they did their best, but I kinda want to learn from some folks that look a lot like me."

"Ya wanna learn from us?" a voice called out, a woman's voice. "'Cause I've got somethin' to say. I'm Skye."

And out stepped this striking woman, with sun-kissed skin and arresting almond eyes, her arms crossed and confident as she stood apart from still-sitting masses. If appearances had to be made, she'd be my vote to represent the unrepresented gathered here. Like Sterling, when she spoke, it was with the will of the people behind her, and I was enamored by it.

"First off, that parable shit is old. Real old. As in, doesn't even apply anymore, that's how old. You really think it's that simple? You get hit, you get paid by the guy who hit ya, and now it's all on you to get back up on your feet, huh?"

All eyes were on me.

All words slipped from my brain.

"Well, it's not," she continued. "Think about it. You get hit, you're down for, what, a few weeks, maybe a few months? Out here, on your own, what happens to your lost income? Mental anguish? Damages to person? You're looking at possibly thousands of dollars meant to come your way, and you *really* think that guy's gonna pay it willingly?

"That's what lawyers are for, man. Lawyers with their words and their papers that can just walk in and make a simple story all convoluted. Now, that driver's lookin' to not pay you a dime. Maybe they get their lawyer to argue on their behalf, maybe the story changes and you were crossing the street when you shouldn't, yeah? And there's no witnesses to corroborate your side. What then? Now you're made out to be the villain, little ol' you in your hurt condition in that hospital room racking up a fortune. What then?"

"It looks pretty bleak," I admitted.

"Except, that's not what we're talkin' about, is it?" she continued. "We're talkin' about if that car hit your great-great-great-grandfather and bankrupted the family. And then his son got hit by a car, and his son, and his son. And by the time the bill comes passed down to you, all those money problems from hit-and-runs gone by, it's so big and so long and so damn overdue you can't even hope to pay it. And you know what then?"

"What?" I asked.

"You file for a massive, just effin enormous pile of money we call *reparations* to even make things remotely square. Ya can't take out a loan from the bank, your credit score was tanked before you were out of diapers, and you need a leg up. And *then,* right when you ask for a little something for your troubles, you're told to not ask for a handout.

"Yeah, it's on us to get here, be here, work our asses off to stay here, and graduate with just a chance at making it out there, but don't for a *second* think that an exception is the same as the rule. All of us on campus are *not* in the same boat. The people that look like us, like you and me, we came in little dinghies trying to weather the storm, and others rolled in on yachts. We. Ain't. The. Same."

You'd be mistaken for passing by that boardroom on a Wednesday evening and thinking you'd missed out on a concert, what with all the cheering after her thorough dressing-down she'd given me. And you'd also be mistaken for thinking it'd really taken the wind out of my sails, my head bowed and eyes down at the floor. But really, if you were like Sterling, with that sly smile and knowing nod, you might've guessed a fire had been lit under me.

"You're right," I said, quietly but forcefully, and enough to silence the room again.

"I talk different, grew up different, but don't think I don't know what it's like to have someone hate you for you are. To not have to put on an act in a professional setting to get hired, to hope... just *hope* they didn't think me a walking stereotype and have to overcompensate the other way. To not have to pretend to go along with it all so I wasn't left behind by it all.

"I guess I know what it's like to be singled out, to be the only one jeered at when everyone else got cheers. Newsflash: they don't stop and ask me if I was adopted into a white family before they toss rocks. They see skin that doesn't look like theirs and they strike."

Deep breaths.

"And that isn't even the experience I remember most. Not when I interviewed the Klansman. Not when I went to New York City, won first place in a worldwide competition for improvisational speaking, and was told I'd only won it because I was Black. Imagine that, telling a little kid proud of their accomplishments they don't deserve it because of their skin color. No, not even then.

"I think about it a lot. Why's it always on me to change when *they're* in the wrong."

People nodded all around the table, which was near silent, save for some shifting up to the edge of seats as I continued.

"So, I get it. I get having to measure every word, watch every act, and be vigilant, always. I get it, because I do it too. That's why I'm so careful not fall into..."

LEARNED HELPLESSNESS

"See, growing up, there was this theory I read about from the University of Pennsylvania: learned helplessness. It's like... there's these elephants, these massive creatures that can rip out of almost anything, and they were kept tied to lampposts at circuses. I used to think, 'Why don't they just rip free?' And you see, they didn't because, in their mind, they *couldn't*. They'd been conditioned from an early age that they couldn't break free from these thick oak trees they were tied to, and so even though they'd grown too far to surpass the strength of any post, their minds were still back to when they were young and couldn't get free."

"What about the most racist thing that ever happened to ya?" a voice from the crowd called. "What about then?"

"That's the thing," I replied. "There's two types of learned helplessness:
- Universal
- Personal

"Universal helplessness is where you feel like there's nothing that can be done about the situation, that there's no way to end it. The other one's got you believing others may be able to find a way out, but we aren't capable of doing it ourselves. That same science says it results in a deficit mindset built into us, one of a few:

- Cognitive
- Motivational
- Emotional

"Cognitive just means we feel our situations are beyond control. Motivational is about us losing the, well, motivation to find our way out... but emotional? *That's* where it gets you so down you get depressed. The most racist thing... well, so far, that I've experienced is applying to college.

"I'm meeting with some staffer who's helping me put together my resume and all, and he sees I'm scoring real low on math. Like, really, real low. I've never been good at it, and it's always been a sore spot for me, but this guy? He takes all that away with one thing he says: 'It's okay to not be great at math; it won't keep you out of college,' and then, that next second, he puts it all back tenfold.

"He tells me, 'It's okay, you're actually higher in your racial demographic so you'll get in. Your demo tends to score lower in those areas anyway. Don't worry about it!'

"I felt... like I was only good 'for a Black,' like I wasn't just bad at math, but I was *expected* to do worse off than others... I never wanted anyone to feel like that again. You're right, you're all right. I don't know a lot about this, but I'm making the effort here, now, to learn more. Nobody knows everything, but we all know something. And I know that we are capable of so much more than we are ever given credit for. *I* know that we can rip our chains off that damn tree!"

And now I could feel the room welcome me. Now, there's claps on the back, a warmness washing over instead of the cold front that greeted me. Skye smiles. Sterling, shockingly, looks surprised, like he can't believe such honesty was so well received. And me? I'm just glad to get through the first few weeks of college.

The soft bigotry of low expectations takes many forms, but for the underrepresented student, it's valuable to understand *why* personal branding is such a great tool. Sticks and stones may break bones, but words can still hurt, and not everyone has a strong sense of self-esteem or support system backing them up—no accountability partners, campus champions, or an affinity group like the Black student union to work with.

But they raise a good point.

Up until now, we've discussed personal branding as self-image, and there still is the systemic lack of opportunities presented to you that remains a problem. As you know, colleges collect social capital, so it's time to start stockpiling.

Let's begin.

2

COLLEGES COLLECT SOCIAL CAPITAL, SO START STOCKPILING

PROFIT IN YOUR POCKET

An investment in knowledge pays the best interest.

BENJAMIN FRANKLIN

KNOWLEDGE ECONOMY

Our founding father makes an interesting point. Knowledge is power and knowing is half the battle. The other half? Applying that to the real world. It stands to reason that the more knowledge you possess, the more power you have to positively impact your pursuits and passions.

"So, hold up. You *actually* said all that? To BSU? 'Rip the damn chains off that tree.' Not bad, kid." Annalise said from the other side of the walkie.

"I'm only a few months younger than you," I said back.

"Same difference."

It's a new semester, a second chance at this whole college thing, and Annalise and I have found ourselves as the resident assistants for our respective halls. The "walkies" we use are technically phones, but they might as well have been archaic radios. A pair of flip-phones with bad coverage and worse reception, they were the designated property of residence life, and besides the brown burlap sack we were forced to carry with campus protocol papers, it was just the two of us stuck inside on a Saturday night.

While the rest of the school celebrated the first week back in the new year, the RAs sit at home, hoping against the odds the phone would not ring for yet another drunk lockout. Still, it gave us time to chat the night away, and that meant story time. She'd come to me with her problems, which I won't share here out of privacy, and I came to her with mine. For the sake of story, we're focusing on the times I leaned on her.

"But yes, Ann, I did say exactly that. What's wrong with what I said?"

"Nothing, nothing. It's just... sorta, kinda totally awesome that you can just recall data like that on the spot. I'd have been terrified they'd eat me alive."

"Yeah, well, an investment in education pays the best interest."

"You keep saying that," she said. "What the heck does that even mean?"

What does it mean indeed? What we're talking now isn't financial capital (that comes later) but the socially-constructed capital that comes from knowing your craft, your industry, and how you can use those knowledge bases to better contribute personally. I refer to it as the **profit in your pocket** we all have but rarely use. Allow me to bring your attention to three words in the quote above:

- *Investment*
- *Knowledge*
- *Interest*

Don't worry; we won't get too technical without explanation. Like we mentioned earlier, colleges are a company, so corporate culture often bleeds into academic speak. The first thing to understand is that this terminology isn't just to sound more legitimate; it has intrinsic value directly correlating to collegiate affairs. When you think of *investment,* you think about money, right? Money can be represented in copper coins, greenbacks, or by the Gold Standard, depending on your monetary system. For higher education, we operate in a knowledge-based or **knowledge economy.** The knowledge economy refers to human capital and the trading of ideas and information contributing to the ebb and flow of innovation. And while Wall Street bankers trade cash, a knowledge economy collects **social capital,** defined by sociologist James Coleman as "the benefits one reaps from intangible resources tied to one's social relationships with others" (Edsurge, 2019).

John Saunders, who was a Wall Street senior vice president for over twenty years, found his point of difference based on advice of a mentor. At twenty-five years old, Saunders felt his career was stalled, passed over for several promotions before his mentor suggested finding volunteer work outside of the firm to expand his skill set. Saunders then met the New York Underground Film Festival director at a party.

"Knowing I wanted to volunteer I asked how they find sponsors. He said they could use help. So we agreed to a commission only structure and I went to work researching, networking and calling."

JOHN SAUNDERS

I believe Saunders's **point of parity** was that he worked on Wall Street. These parity points are aspects of your identity that put you on the list of qualified persons for a school, job, or other opportunity, kind of like meeting the prerequisite requirements that put you in the running for a race. Points of parity are like the "you-must-be-this-tall-to-ride" for life like how jobs require a bachelor's degree and a few years' experience for an entry-level job. It's the thing you need to even qualify for a position... kind of defeating the purpose of it being *entry* level in my opinion, but I digress.

Even then, Saunders could not just advance as wanted, what with everyone in his firm more than likely following the same pattern with the same points of parity. No, he had to go outside the norm, find a **point of difference** that put him above the competition, diversify his skill set, and, building off our personal brand talk, establish himself as "that guy" easily remembered in the office.

That's the power of social capital in action. Saunders needed leverage, and instead of jumping at the sheer rock face that was the corporate ladder, he took a detour through the arts and gained some **transferable experiences**: outside involvement in one aspect of life that can intersect and aid you in another. Us college students and hopefuls recognize this, if not by name, then by principle.

THE PERMISSION PARADOX

To get a job after college you need experience, but in order to get experience you need a job, trapping you in a penniless, jobless runaround. To "buy" your way out of this, heck, to "buy" your way into college on the application, you must stock up on social capital, leading us back to a very important question.

What is investment?

Here, it relates to the idea of **relational trust.** In education, that's the level of safety afforded between student and teacher, student and school, and student to the wider educational system they are a part of. EL Education reports this relational trust as capitalizing on interpersonal social exchanges in the classroom setting. If you're wondering about the strength of your relational capacity, ask yourself these questions:

- Do you trust your teacher is competent in their course?
- Is the assigned classwork challenging enough for your grade level?
- Is it *too* challenging for your grade level?
- Do you believe your school adequately sets you up for future success?

This is student capacity, the improvement of your own skills in connection with the given curriculum. By "building capacity," the educational ecosystem thrives. When applying to college in your last years of high school, does your institution:

- Make scholarship opportunities accessible?
- Ensure you are prepared for the standardized testing needed?
- Pride itself on a faculty and professional staff able and willing to facilitate your growth into higher education?

Interest in education is really tied to a **return on investment,** the measure of worth undertaking an activity is. A good public or private school should help you get into a good college or job, with both hoping to earn you considerably more money than if you hadn't joined up with them. Otherwise, what's the point? This relational trust is built off that social capital, and is best signified as a formula:

Return on Investment = Net Profit / Cost of Investment
or
ROI= Good College, Better Job / Cost of College

Your ROI will differ from others, but you can quickly calculate your odds here. College majors are all equal, but some fields of study are more equal and pay more handsomely than others. As a proud liberal arts degree holder, my ROI equation does not have Harvard's tuition in the "cost of college" section, in no small part due to the high price of the schooling possibly not worth it when other institutions offer similar degrees for much less. But that's my personal decision and yours to make, too.

A school's social capital is determined by their relational trust built upon the positive return on investments from students who've gone there. We only recognize places like Princeton University and University of Pennsylvania for the successful alumni, amenities afforded by going there, and the likelihood that some of the magic might rub off on us, right?

Well, be aware there is a dark side to social capital, as much like any other industry, there are charlatans. Unfortunately, us underserved students might chomp at the first bit we get, and that's exactly what these kinds of scammers like to do. While nobody we know of course would fall for any Nigerian princes asking for money, there may be a few that'd fall for a school that *guaranteed* students' admission into prominent four-year institutions.

This is the cautionary tale of an FBI investigation into an account of academic abuse, admissions fraud, and physical harassment of Black students at a Louisiana prep school.

This is the story of "Nelson and Blake."

ACADEMIC ABUSE

———

You don't know their names, but you might've heard their story.

See, college isn't just a cut above your current schooling; we've made it into a cultural phenomenon here in the US. Remember those acceptance letter YouTube videos, with kids opening letters from Cornell, Boston, and New York Universities, surrounded by their cheering classmates? Those went viral, especially when a Louisiana-based college preparatory school stole the national spotlight with its 100 percent acceptance rate to four-year institutions, including the three listed above. In fact, *The New York Times* reported an eight-million-times-viewed video starring the school where underprivileged Black students got accepted into top-tier colleges. It's a regular Cinderella story.

If only the book closed there.

The plot twisted violently in 2018, where *The New York Times* penned a follow-up to the success story, sparking an investigation into allegations of abuse, lies, and mistreatment of the student body. The college prep was founded and ran by a former salesman-turned-teacher and his wife, a nurse-now-principal of the preparatory, who stood accused of beating, choking, and forcing kids to kneel for hours as punishment. Though court ordered to anger management and found guilty of simple battery, the crime most covered in the account was the doctoring of college applications. Students were sworn to secrecy, forbid from discussing school-related activity with their parents, something Nathan believes is why the leaders of the Louisiana school could lead the world on for so long. I spoke with him to get his version of the story.

"A story's right!" Nelson told me. "They trafficked in 'sob stories.' They stooped to stereotypes and gave us all poor backgrounds and abusive households even when we didn't have them. They told us it was the only way we'd get into the schools of our choice looking the way we did and coming from the place we came from. We had to play to their sympathies, because, as he said, 'You sure aren't gonna play to your smarts.' Story sells, he'd always say."

Story sells.

He didn't think of himself as the kind of kid to flock to a cult school (his words, not mine), but that relational trust, built off the knowledge this Louisianan school boasted a 100 percent acceptance rate to four-year institutions, proved too potent to pass up from his parents. They overlooked the late hours, the secrecy, and the allegations from students. Nelson even accepted the school's founder, a thought leader of radical ideology, including a disbelief in the autism spectrum.

"I was living proof it existed, and he didn't care," Nelson said. "No special circumstances. No 'handouts,' as he put it. I'm on the spectrum, so what I needed wasn't a handout; it was a necessity. I wasn't even allowed to retreat to a room by myself to read, rather that I should constantly be intermingled with a crowd so that I'd 'get used to' all the noise. Our principal didn't believe in disability."

Nelson remembers his principal stating, "'If you're going to beat those Blacks, you're gonna have to be better than this!' He pulled this act on a big meeting with the elementary to middle school kids, pointing out two to three white students that were outperforming the rest of the class. There wasn't as much 'white versus Black' as there was 'Black versus white,' much more often about 'Don't let this white kid beat you' when the sentiment was vocalized."

Oh yeah, this "thought leader"was also a race-baiter.

And that's on top of the doctoring documents to get his students into college, or the forced kneeling for hours as punishment. When word finally broke out, the relational trust the leader and the school built up on the backs of parents' goodwill and seemingly positive outcomes was shattered, not just with the student base, but with the colleges involved, too. Should Stanford and Princeton have seen through this? What other instances of fraud have slipped through the proverbial cracks? Much like the Harvard admissions scandal, each incident speaks to a growing concern: can we still place our faith in these institutions?

How it relates back to you: When applying to schools and you definitely, totally, certainly get in, you're not entirely off the hook. Social capital can work against you if you're not careful, even after you've received that letter of acceptance.

1. Poor academic performance
2. Disciplinary action
3. Abhorrent online activity

In a knowledge economy, investment goes both ways, with colleges asking themselves if *you* can be trusted to fulfill investment on your end. If, after acceptance, your grades slip from A's to C's and D's, you might get a warning mailed your way, or a reneging on the next four years of your life if a few F's find their way to your report card.

Any sort of suspension, and certainly an expulsion, can put you in jeopardy of changing your chances, so no brawls in the halls or getting caught where you should not. And with everything online, please refrain from posting what might not impress professionals on your public profile. Any compromising photos, crude language, or otherwise questionable content on a public forum can and will be sought after by admissions teams. Implicit bias can also play a role. Even if unknowingly, I'd hate for something so small to have such a large and negative impact on your chances.

Then there's knowledge itself. You ever hear about the "ghost in the machine"? The philosopher that posited that, Gilbert Ryle, was an Oxford philosopher who also broke down knowledge into four distinct categories:

1. *Know-what,* focusing on the accumulation of factual information and evidence. This is most closely linked to the cite-your-sources kind of intelligence.

2. *Know-who,* referring to social interactions and how they can, for example, fit into an ideal team to produce optimal results. This is the one you'll need most to get into college, and is supported by

3. *Know-how,* the work-with-your-hands experience needed to physically get the work done. Think blue-collar, outdoors, and machinery work that requires application of principles in a practical purpose.

4. *Know-why,* the implementation of theoretical study for mass innovation. In order to create new ideas, we need adequate background knowledge on what's come before.

In the knowledge economy, we've shifted the focus from job searching after high school to the college search. Who else grew up with parents *insisting* you'd attend university, all in the service of gainful employment down the line? I know I did, and despite being first in the family to do so, I was raised as if it was just the next logical step in my livelihood. A difficult, costly step, but inevitable, nonetheless.

Through a college degree, I'd trade out some full-time work experience for the academic know-how to land a (hopefully) higher-paying job. And you know one of the first things I learned? It's not just *what* you know or *who* you know, but *how* you can use what you know to great effect.

Founder and CEO of Universal Data Basic Income (UBDI) agrees. You don't know her? You're about to. And how you use that information is up to you.

INTEREST OVER TIME

Remember when Facebook founder Mark Zuckerberg was called to testify before Congress about people's private data being traded? Yeah, that's what Budzyn's company is trying to solve: giving control back to the customers.

> *"We're trying to merge privacy and profit to create a universal basic data income. Facebook is valuable not just because of the data they collect, but because you're there too. If you leave, the data doesn't bring them any more money."*
>
> DANA BUDZYN

This can be applied to colleges, and why brand names of schools get tossed around so much in higher education. They're only as important as the people going there, and that's why the brand built behind your name is so bankable—that and finding ways to capitalize on your social capital.

Budzyn conquers amidst a culture of venture capitalists. The former NASA Jet Propulsion Laboratory intern and TEDx speaker launched herself to the forefront with UBDI and with her induction into the Female Founder Collective.

All this, and she still wants to make something very clear about the road to success:

> *"Us entrepreneurs hear a lot about the Pelotons of the world, the go-getters who got four hundred no's before the yes that made them who they are today... if I could get into four hundred rooms, I'd happily accept. A more realistic reality is dealing with someone going through a checklist of items and looking for that 'perfect story,' which most startups don't have, that gets you stopped at the door."*
>
> DANA BUDZYN

Budzyn recalls one room she was let into, and how somewhere between 2–3 percent of investment funds go into minority-fronted projects, including that of women and underrepresented racial groups. Instead of splitting a large pie evenly among the founders coming to the table, it was as if one small slice was then further split in two for her and others to fight over, rather than actively drawing from all available resources.

Maybe it's my American upbringing, but I've grown really tired of the "rugged individualism" storyline that gets passed around. You know what I'm talking about—the stories of folks described as *self-made* and "pulling themselves up by their bootstraps." It's not to say they didn't rightfully earn where they are, but did they really get there on their own?

I'll use myself as an example. I didn't get to college all on my own. Sure, my grades showed work ethic and my extracurriculars spotlight my personality and drive, but I couldn't have visited any campus without my parents driving me or known how to fill out the application without mentors from high school. Even other classmates whose parents had gone to college gave some insight into how to best navigate the labyrinth of academia, leading me to where I am today. If not for them, I wouldn't be writing this book at all! Sociologist James Coleman saw social capital as *the benefits one reaps from the intangible resources tied to one's social relationships with others.* Ever had someone put in a good word for you? If you're a college student reading this, I know you had to ask somebody to write you a recommendation letter. The idea behind the letter is to get an unbiased but favorable view of you from a manager or someone else who has worked with you before, preferably in your field of study. It's a critical component meant to act as a character witness and vouch on your "I'm sure you mentioned because why wouldn't you" skill set like time management and personal accountability. A few things to note:

DO ask an experienced academic professional and/or someone well versed in your area of expertise.

DO NOT ask family or friends, as their impartial status in relation to you implies bias, negating any positives they highlight for you as favoritism.

DO emphasize relationships over rank. A C-suite executive may look better vouching for you on paper, but be sure they actually know your name. The more personal the professional connection is, the more honest and helpful the letter can be. This relates back to having that strong personal branding to ensure they've got good things to say about you.

Let's examine students A and B.

Student A: A soon-to-be communications major who requests his church pastor to pen his letter of recommendation.

Student B: An expected physics major who nabs a NASA aeronautics engineer to write his recommendation letter.

I know what you're thinking: Those are two rather extreme examples, no? And yes, they are. They're also true. I went to high school with students A and B, where B's family was involved with NASA assignments for years, and so their only child had up close and personal time with some of the nation's top physicists in that field of study. Student A isn't completely out of the running yet, but they'll have to make some changes to level the playing field:

- Rank and relationship: Establish strong, natural bonds with your mentors in internships and job sites so as to have those with influence back your dreams and have that closeness to make it all the more real.
- Transferable experience: A lot of resume building is quite literally building off all you've done before. Two people with the same experiences can look very different on the page, and that all comes down to is translating your relevant experiences accurately.

Over time, you can start to collect the social capital from these "assets" you've acquired, and then, you can build interest.

"Ugh, social capital," Annalise bemoaned on the other end of the line, the phone connecting us as we completed our individual rounds, circling the empty corridors of our residence halls. "It's all about who you know, who knows you, and who cares *what* you know! It's just so frustrating to see these people with an inside connection get streamlined through the process. Nepotism! That's the word for it. 'Family gets in for free!'"

"That's definitely one way to look at it," I admitted. "I grew up in a small town. Politics was just the price to pay to play, so to speak. But up here? Yeah, totally different ballgame. There's rooms I'm not let into, and even more I don't know about."

"Right? And, you know I hate playing the race card, so I won't. But someone else could say being a minority has its drawbacks sometimes."

"Sometimes?"

"Sometimes. Not here to make it all about race or gender, just saying there's definitely levels of engagement from higher-ups, and maybe we're not at the topmost level, you know?"

"I do," I said.

But I didn't. Well, I had an idea.

If investment ties to relational capacity, and knowledge ties to a knowledge-based economy, interest refers to what you get out of all of this by day's end. I mean, that's the goal, right? Remember the permission paradox? In order to get a job, you need experience... except that for you to get any experience, you're going to need that job. Interest is having that social capital accrue over time, so, upon graduation, you've formed the right network to leverage what social capital you've captured before to "cash in," utilizing both what and who you know to make that leap into your professional field. How do you build this interest?

- Solve an issue
- Provide a service
- Create an experience

1. I always say I'm not smart, but pretty damn clever. Someone can memorize a textbook and recite it word for word, and hey, good for them. Me? I'm more inclined to condense the information, turning a novel into a notepad. If you find inventive ways in your career to make the job easier, you'll have your point of difference defined for yourself.

2. Another way is providing a service. I first joined my undergraduate institution as a tour guide, then resident

assistant, then orientation leader, all before I became an academic tutor. After offering academic advice for two years, I expanded into career course correction as well, providing an online service to help students adjust to life changes and personal development while on campus. I leveraged my already-firm positions to lend credibility and legitimacy to my operations as an independent consultant.

3. Creation of anything is also impressive. It alludes to an innovative mindset, which gives the impression you think outside the box, which is *exactly* the kind of fresh, new talent colleges seek and the correlation you want them to make with you. Every applicant has a high school diploma, a few extracurriculars, and maybe an AP class or two. Not all can claim they have provided real-world solutions to real-world problems.

Come on, even on paper that sounded good.

So, interest, knowledge, and investment—a knowledge economy run on social capital and understanding all its components can only help you navigate academia. Did you know there was more than one type of social capital? Think of it like various forms of fiat money, like dollar bills, coins, and checks. In our case, we have:

- Bonding
- Bridging
- Linking

Bonding: what brings people together. If you and a classmate both play a particular sport, and a teacher also doubles as that sport's coach, that bond through a shared activity yields social capital. Look for what unites rather than divides people, and you'll find yourself with enough possible recommendations that you needn't worry.

Bridging: This requires you to step outside of your comfort zone a little. Maybe you're not as close to people at work, your internship, or your least favorite extracurricular. But by strengthening those bonds, you'll expand your **spheres of influence (SOI)**. Think of them as your circles of trust you have where you and others have influence over one another. These near peers create **peer-to-peer networking** opportunities, or the trading of ideas, information, and resources. Simply put, think of that one classmate in one class you don't talk to outside of, but you always ask if there was any homework assigned.

We've all got to stick together.

Linking: This is where we separate the average from the A students. Linking requires you to completely leave your entrenched spheres of influence and expand to spark new ones. The best way to complete this is to find professionals in your industry on LinkedIn for a cold call, using any mutual connections to help break the ice. Who knows, it just might land you that dream job right out of college.

"Yeah, maybe," Annalise agreed. "'Course, you're forgetting to account for a few things. Surprised you didn't bring up **social exchange theory**. This idea that all of us are connected through our social relationships. You know how they say, 'You're the sum of your five best friends'?"

I was familiar. You get shown around a college; the physical tradeoff is shown in the amenities, the state-of-the-art gym, or indoor pool. In social exchanges, it's knowing that Pulitzer Prize-winning professor just might teach your class, or the former NFL athlete-turned-coach might have some connections in the sports media world you can benefit from.

"Yeah?" I said.

"Well, we're not. I mean, we are, but we are so much more than that. We're the five closest friends, and their closest friends, and their acquaintances, and it's just this ever-expanding spider web that can have wide-reaching impact. It's who you know, remember?"

"So you're saying the Six Degrees of Kevin Bacon has some educational value?"

"Ha. Ha. But, yeah, I guess I am. If you track degrees of separation and see how people are connected, isn't it strange the people in power always know each other? *Nepotism!*"

"Lotta closed-door meetings in rooms we're not invited into."

"Exactly! And that **relational aggression** keeps the outsiders out. I'm talking badmouthing, favoritism, clique creations, all that back-stabbing BS."

"You don't gotta tell me about this... relational aggression, you called it? I've plenty of experience with that."

"Why do I feel this is another Noah story coming on?"

"Because it kinda, sorta, totally is... but only if you're interested."

I hear an overly dramatic sigh through the phone. "You know I do."

"I swear, this one's educational. It's totally on topic. Lemme tell you about how you can use social capital to get ahead in school."

"Okay, professor. Class is in session."

"I mean, unless you don't want to hear about how I accidentally got our high school principal and superintendent fired, that is."

"START THE DANG STORY!"

THE MOMENTS THAT MAKE US

Understand that as a snotty high school sophomore, I wasn't nearly as impassioned with education as I am now. In fact, I didn't want to get involved at all!

I wanted to get the heck out of that four-walled prison cell called a classroom into the great unknown. Whatever it was, it had to be better than the place that required permission to use the bathroom and classes on subjects you never needed again. I didn't skip classes, paid attention, raised my hand, but each day felt like the last and I was counting down the days until summer started. But it's the *one* day you miss when everything happens, right? Well, this was one of *those* days, involving a firing, a lawsuit, a DUI, a resignation, and a massive protest on school property.

Oh, and I was in class that day... I'm kind of responsible for it.

Suddenly, school got exciting and maybe you'd call it bravery, or moxie, or whatever it was that gives me the strength to say the things I say and do the things I do—though some might call it grit.

And maybe a year or two ago, I would've called it that, too.

Angela Duckworth, American psychologist and award-winning author, defined grit in her aptly-titled book *Grit: The Power of Passion and Perseverance* as just that: passion and perseverance for long-term and meaningful goals (Fessler, 2018). She puts a focus not on the in-the-moment emotion, but on the commitment and consistency it takes to see actions to completion.

During the 2017 NAACP Image Awards, Denzel Washington, one of my idols, addressed the cheering crowd with an awesome mantra to live by:

> *Without commitment, you'll never start... and without consistency, you'll never finish.*

Duckworth comments, "Without grit, talent may be nothing more than unmet potential." Like before, this grit isn't about "trying harder" or setting unrealistically high expectations (see: high skill floor) for yourself. Instead, it's about applying what we discussed into action.

And yet, what I'd always called grit was really persistence, as Dr. Yolanda Norman would say. An educational consultant and first-generation college student researcher, she defines persistence as the continuity of effort. Grit, while I love Duckworth's definition, can unfortunately be co-opted by the powers that be to have a similar connotation to the "pulled up by your own bootstraps" mentality, which doesn't address one's individual circumstances. Persistence, Norman claims, is a more functional term for an ambitious student who perseveres past all obstacles.

She finds the difference between persistence and retention to be an important one. Persistence places focus on the students' efforts being made to better themselves in an academic environment, while retention is a term institutions use to quantify the lived experiences of students who remain committed to college year after year. Retention includes the numbers, but leaves out persistence, the personal data of how and why they stayed. For underrepresented students, though, talk of grit is often used to explain why if they just try harder, opportunities will open themselves up.

EQUALITY VERSUS EQUITY.
Back then, creative writing was my career to be (and here we are!), so I was enjoying the only class I really enjoyed, AP English, when the PA system screeched to life.

"Today is Mr. Stonewall's last day. We'd like to all wish you a happy retirement and a thank you for your years of service!"

My high school just lost one of its best principals, an ex-football coach in favor with the community off to enjoy his golden years after spending his best ones with us. The transition had been a long time coming, the delicate balance of urbanity bound together by feeble policies and a below-par disciplinarian. A toothless tiger took the place of the once-proud lionized leader, and the animals of the academic community took note. Let me ask:

- Should you destroy class projects after hours?
- Or start an underground fight club during lunch hour?
- What about destroying personal property during all the other hours?

If you gave a definite answer to any of these questions, then I'm sorry, my high school at the time just wasn't for you.

And you'd better not need the bathroom when at school, because we had none... okay, we did, but we had them locked twenty-four seven. Several crappy situations found their way onto the walls, and the custodians (rightfully so) got tired of cleaning up biological waste. Administration stepped in, enforcing the "tough call" to close bathroom use without having an office aid walk you to the lavatory, key in hand, and wait for you outside while you handled your business. So, not entirely off limits, but you can imagine the everyday kid avoiding the experience if at all possible.

The smarter kids wouldn't bother with lockers either since, ah, they didn't *lock*. Blades were bartered at the battlegrounds for fight club, and before long the lockers lost their namesake clasps. Knives were nested away, and thieves took to thieving. Best to keep your belongings in your backpack on your back at all times.

But besides that, great place we had there.

Seriously though, the teachers made going there bearable. By this point, I'd given up football for theater, trading out my two-a-day practices for all-nighters on the theater set. These "work parties" could span hours, from right after school up to ten at night. We had our friends, we had our homework, and teachers were generally understanding. I loved every minute of it. But preparing for production is painful, and we were going into Hell Week. Call it "Technical" or "Tech Week," that last few days before the play became professional were hours of line readings, light cues, and exhausted teens struggling to get through take after take after take of the same scene, shifting a little more each time. Call it whatever you want; there's a reason "Hell" is up there.

That's when it was announced we'd received our new principal, and an assembly was formed to greet him in the main auditorium. That meant the set had to be hidden behind the red curtain and the theater kids were off duty—just two of the reasons I could breathe a sigh of relief walking from backstage to the front, joining a class eager to do anything outside of the classroom. The rest of us sophomores sat in the middle rows while seniors flocked to the rear and freshmen huddled in the front. And there on stage, a solo act save for a single microphone stand, was our combat veteran-turned-school savior.

Let's call him... Stonewall. Principal Stonewall's tall frame cast long shadows offstage, an imposing figure far rounder in the middle than broader in the shoulders. He shuffled his feet where others would've stepped, though I'd attribute that to his age. He looked about mid-fifties in the face but a decade more behind deadened eyes and slowed movements. Perhaps he was a soldier once, perhaps too much, now a hollowed shell of the warrior within. He willed himself toward the microphone where out croaked the hoarsest whisper that barely reached the third row.

"I'm Mr. Stonewall. I'm here today to introduce myself as your new principal. I'm Mr. Stonewall." He repeated, lost his way for a second, then continued.

"As some of you know, I served this country for many years. I'm proud of this country, and I'm proud of its youth— of all of you."

So far so good, right? No points for style and a little wandering at times, but nothing too overtly abnormal. And then, for reasons I still can't comprehend, he made his father the focal point of his featured moment.

"My dad's dead. Been dead for years. And you know... he died alone. Old, friendless, and alone. That's because he didn't have friends. Me? I have friends. I have all of you. And as long as we are friends, I do not have to fear dying old and alone... because we are all friends here."

Arms out, an embrace to all accepted by none, and alone and seemingly unafraid (though his students were),

Stonewall stayed fixed in place like a frozen animation as a little English teacher took the microphone and stole back the horrific scene.

"Ah... um... t-thank you, Mr. Stonewall. Everyone give Mr. Stonewall a big hand!"

And she's clapping as she's holding the microphone, its feedback flashing on the faces of the recoiling students. A sudden outcry masks the spread of red across her face as she nervously edges Stonewall off stage left. We're clustered out the back moments after, a gaggle of gossip for a grand total of five minutes, and then it's back to what's for terrible lunch. I remember a distinct discomfort, a feeling your finger couldn't fit on but crept up your arm and down your spine. I didn't recognize it as *lack of faith in authority figure* because, until then, you're entirely dependent on them. What's not to trust?

As I would find, there was very much not to trust.

Defacement and destruction of school devices continued, with doors barred and dead-bolted against the delinquents outside, who dart up and down the halls. That day's class was accompanied by the crashing and cluttering of lockers' contents across the floor, a code of conduct cleanly out of sight. It wasn't total anarchy, Stonewall said, but controlled chaos, a manageable mayhem he deemed "not worthy of personal intervention." In his world, the strong didn't just survive, but thrived on the misfortune of those deemed weak. In a sense, there was no management of expectations. It was pretty bad when Crystal, a student representative, showed more discipline than the disciplinarian.

Crystal served on the school board, the folks that ran all things scholarly in our central Pennsylvanian school in Smalltown, Pennsylvania. They're based over at the Island

Park Administrative Office, which is neither on an island or in a park, and comprised of an all-volunteer, upper- to middle-class body. Unlike them, Crystal recognized the rampant raucousness plaguing the halls had driven up the number of cyber students, but technical issues remained unresolved weeks into the semester.

"Look, these online kids... they just wanna check their grades, right? If the board would just, like, release their report cards like they want, poof, we're all cool. They're cool. I'm cool. Everyone's cool." Amber said this as we sat on the steps leading to the stage, set-building and line-practicing behind us and drowning out our conversation as she continued.

"I think they just don't wanna admit they're wrong."

"Definitely."

"Like, they've made the decision to use this program, it backfired, and now they don't wanna admit they made a mistake."

"Yup."

"Which is childish!"

"I agree!"

"But," she sighed, that fighting spirit slowed for a second. "But what the hell can we do besides complain to the board? I'm like, the only one who brings it up every week, and every week I'm told to just sit down and keep my mouth shut and ears open. That this is an opportunity for me to learn through observation... basically, I'm a PR stunt, not actually there to make a difference. And hell, why would I? Only, like, five people show up to these meetings every week. Nobody cares, so why should they?"

I had an idea.

"You get to discuss current events, right?"

"Yeah, there's 'Public Comment' for the general public, 'Student Speak' for, ya know, me, and the board talks about whatever's on their agenda and current events. Why?"

A bright bulb of an idea lit up my smile, and before I got the words out, I could see her return it in kind; we were on the same page.

"I think, if there were a current event they'd *have* to discuss, that got the public's interest, and you were informed on, we could get this information out there! You want the cyber students to get some attention; I want the discipline issue addressed. Both of these are because Stonewall isn't doing his job. If we come together—"

"The board will *have* to listen! Especially if people make sure they're aware!"

From my point of view, she had a voice on the council when there was talk of the town, and I had a problem needing to be solved. I'd supply the message, and Crystal would deliver it. Grit means taking matters into our own hands. And while I didn't mean it literally, there I was the next day, the cafeteria microphone in hand, explaining:

"Mr. Stonewall says there's no problem here, but he hasn't had a project destroyed or his stuff stolen. He hasn't been locked out of restrooms because of some few. Heck, he's roaming the halls with them! Why are we being punished for the actions of others?"

And would you *believe* the microphone was ripped from my hands? Apparently, the assistant principal didn't appreciate my student activism, but the students made up for it with their energized applause, a surge coursing through the cafe even as I was none-so-gently escorted out of the lunchroom towards the main office. My "little stunt," as Stonewall called it, attracted a few protests just outside school property, so as not to be banned. One spark ignites another, and then my little fires of passion caught wind and were carried across the classrooms as I faced the red-hot fury of a vengeful veteran.

"You should've come to me first," he said.

"With all due respect, sir, I did."

"And? What did I tell you?"

"You said I was, and I quote, 'shooting sparrows with a cannon.'"

"Don't quote me, boy. I know what I said."

"Even though I think it's more like arrows at a tank at this point, sir."

"Don't!" he sighed, composed himself, then continued. "You really think this... little stunt you pulled, all this, what's going on in the halls... is that big of a deal?"

"As I'm sure you know, sir, one person's freedom ends where another's begins. When personal property gets damaged, grades get affected, and safety isn't secure, I do think that is a big deal. And, if I'm being honest, I think it's your job to keep that from happening. We've got parents, students, and teachers all talking about the same issues, and when students are asking for more accountability, I think that's a sign—"

"Enough!" He stood so fast the chair flew back and he stormed to his phone. I saw stubby fingers stab at numbers.

I thought for sure I'd see flashing red and blue, but no, it got worse.

"You wanna play principal? Tell me how to do my job? Fine. Why not head over to the Island and tell *the Chairman* your little story?"

I... purposefully neglected to tell one part of the story. Right before the Board brought on Stonewall, they got his name from the superintendent they just hired, the Chairman.

I mean, he has a real name, but I'm not getting sued from a guy I helped get fired, so we'll call him the Chairman since he never left his. He was an old college buddy of Stonewall's, and even though the veteran spent more time muttering to himself while wandering the halls instead of running the school, what could go wrong? When Stonewall phoned him up about the Noah situation, he realized exactly what could go wrong, and insisted on handling the matter.

Personally.

A hop, skip, and a twenty-minute jump in the car over to the Island I went, ushered into the office of the Chairman himself. I'd never seen such snarly secretaries before, with their lips curled and eyes slanted, so I slid on by in silence. Around the bend of office cubicles stood an open oak door leading to a conference room, one seemingly impossibly long table with the large, padded chair of the Chairman at the far end, and a plastic foldup for me at the other.

I took a seat.

The bald, brawny bulwark of a boss, whose icy blue eyes betrayed a burgeoning grudge just behind his "benign" smile, sat still, silent, and quiet as I waited in the speechless space, both awaiting the other to move first. He may have been playing strategically, hoping I'd show weak points with an opening argument. Me? I was more thrown off by his Cheshire grin and the lack of a formal introduction. Remember, this is the CEO of all the schools in the area, the guy you'd want to write your recommendation letter, not be written up to. As the red hand of the clock above him whirred into its first minute, he broke his own code.

"As I understand it, you have a problem with the way I run my district."

"Well, sir, I—"

"Let me stop you there. Do you wish to run this district?"

"N-No, sir, if I can just—"

"Good, good. That's very good. Because you are many years and several degrees away from doing so. You need both, and a damned good sense for management. All of that can be chalked up to experience, which I have two decades of to reference for why I make the decisions I do. This compared to your... how many now?"

"... none, sir."

"None. Correct." Cold, calculated, critical, a career of cutting programs and creating budgets left him stony and cynical as he leaned in close to make his point clear. "I've been doing this a long time. Longer than you've been around. We all have. All of us here. We care for you, provide for you, and teach you how to make it in this world. Unless you're fixing to run your complaints up to *my* superiors on the school board, I'd strongly advise you pack your things, return to class, and appreciate the education your parents are paying for. Now, will there be any concerns to address, Mr...?"

"Fenstermacher. It's Noah Fenstermacher, sir," I said as I stood up, a confidence rising in me from some place within I'd not yet known. "And yes, there are. You'll be hearing about them from me at the school board meeting this Thursday."

I don't know where the fire under my seat got lit, maybe it just burned me up to think I could get shut down like that. For the first time, a bushy eyebrow raised from my owlish antagonist, though I'd already stormed out to my car and had her in drive before I could witness the first drop of sweat anxiously drip down the Chairman's face.

That Thursday, a few hours before the school board meeting, I was ready for him to remember my name.

At the moment, I was just another student in physics class, struggling to understand the relatively simple equations on the board. Math and science were interesting to me, but it was English and the social sciences that held my attention. So when our teacher requested I step out into the hall—that someone asked for me—I was more relieved than wondering who it was, and astonished to find the Chairman in wait.

See, right before he came for me, he'd already gone after Crystal. We'd just split up from our last-minute planning session in the theater, going over the last of the details.

"You've got the students for sure coming?" she asked.

"You know it. And they're bringing their parents along too. Enough's enough, and I'm hoping the show of force of just seeing the community gathered might be enough to get a response from the board. How's it coming with the teachers?"

"They're ready. Like you said, they've had enough, and we have actual evidence supporting our claims, so we can just hammer away at all the issues we have. This... this might actually work."

"It definitely will. It has to."

"Only problem I see is we have about... two hundred?! You got two hundred people to show? Jeez, well, the building's only got enough seats for, like, seventy people. Max."

"Then we'll make room. Or people will stand, bring chairs, whatever. Something's gotta give and I'd rather it be building capacity than our school system."

"Well, when you put it like that." She clapped her notebook shut as the bell rang for next period. "See you afterward?"

"You bet."

And then, right after we'd parted ways was when the Chairman vacated his ivory office and made for the high school, or more specifically, the principal's office. The office has a CCTV system set up to monitor all activity in public spaces, though the Chairman found it helpful for his personal use. Stalking us throughout the day, he'd trailed by after each class to interrogate each teacher about our whereabouts, and by fifth period he'd tracked Crystal down to the hallway leading out the back of the theater. Without a word, he'd ripped her notebook from her hands, and dashed off back to the safety of the main office. After reading, he made his way to physics, knowing I'd be there, to finish the intimidation audit he'd started.

"I'm aware of what you are doing."

"I already told you what I was doing... sir."

"Don't talk back! I know you're going to the school board tonight and I know who's all gonna be there. So you'd best just tell me. What. Are. You. *Doing*?"

He was nose to nose with me, and I practically whispered back, "*accountability.*"

"Everything alright out here?"

It was my physics teacher! She left class to address the obviously-tense stare down outside her door, and the peer pressure put the Chairman in an unenviable spot.

"No problem. Just... checking in with a student," he claimed, backing down the hall with tail between his legs. "Nothing to worry about, just get back to class... now."

It would be the last time I'd see the Chairman, chair or no chair.

My mob of well-meaning marchers met at the Island office, all 252 of us to be exact, a conglomerate of concerned kids, parents, and their teachers, with a rabble of reporters ready for the ruckus and a collection of complaints spanning the semester.

I spoke in front of the community.

I agreed to an interview with the school board president.

I read about my exploits in the local newspaper the next day.

In all, the Chairman turned out to be a paranoid person, someone so afraid of getting caught he ensured his own downfall. A DUI charge in New York haunted him, and after our meeting last week, he believed I couldn't have had the courage to stand up to him, say the things I said and do the things I did, without some dirt on him.

I didn't.

I went in there armed only with the truth, of wrongs that needed righted, and a cause that needed carried out. My mom, still a custodian at the time, was encouraging but nervous. I wanted to make sure the words spoken were my own, and that nobody there would take out the actions of one loud kid on his hardworking mother.

"Everything I said, everything I'm doing here, is all of my own volition," I said. "My mother is here with me tonight, supporting me—but as my mother. I want to say this because I'm afraid. I'm afraid any blow back for my actions might affect her. That's why I'm saying this now, for everyone to hear: My mom's a hard-working woman, and for anyone who has a problem with me... to take it up with me. Not anyone else."

I tell that story every time I'm asked, "What made you want to go into the field of higher education?"

These are moments that make us.

Barb Short, the former chief diversity officer and president of the PSEG Foundation, spoke at the 2019 International Corporate Citizenship Conference. While there, Short described the importance of **social disruptors:** agents of change within an organization or industry that can make positive and seismic shifts in the field for the better.

> *"We took the 'expert's' advice and were nearly bankrupt in a year, but bounced back due to our own estimations. The people we look to for a stamp of validation know a lot, but not everything. We were asked, 'Why should we invest in such a young founder?' I don't know, maybe because we're young, creative, and not caught in a bubble of hand-shaking and empty gestures!"*
>
> DANA BUDZYN

And now she's launched a company covered by *The New York Times, Business Insider,* and *USA Today,* a true social disruptor having positive impact in her field.

In fact, there are a few things social disruptors are good for:

- Adaptable: the direct response to phrases like, "We've always done it this way." When you enter new academic and work environments, *positive* social disruptors make forward leaps and bounds to stay relevant and useful. Adapt to survive, especially in academia.
- Innovative: When relational capacity and trust is built, you are given new opportunities. Finding ways to help as a tutor or teaching assistant grants you closer proximity to deciding powers and where you can impact the way things are done and how, helping you and your resume.
- Necessary: More than just being a good student, college is about becoming the person you want to be, and a stand-up individual stands against oppressive and unfair conditions, no matter how difficult.

This is one example I wish I wouldn't have to highlight.

See, around the same time Annalise and I chatted it up into the late hour, patrolled empty halls, and broke up the occasional after-hours altercation, there was one resident of mine having an even longer night. Kaitlyn Tempalsky, a neuroscience major and sorority member, waited up for a call that would never come.

Her boyfriend, Tim Piazza, was at another school in his own Greek organization, enjoying his weekend with friends. As part of the organization's idea of a good time, members were forced to drink an exorbitant amount of alcohol, a game they play until fraternity men could not physically handle any more. Piazza played this game, egged on by the others, and passed out at the top of the stairs. In the madness and mayhem of the night's party, Piazza's unconcious body was knocked down the stairs, dragged back up, then knocked down again, causing irreparable damage to his internal organs.

Nine-one-one was never called.

Witnesses say a single friend attempted to intervene and was physically forced away. As late night subsided into early morning, the fraternity members were faced with the fallout of their friend's fate, the battered and bruised boy now beyond their reach. Sadly, the biggest surprise of all was that this was not accounted for sooner, as the organization had a history of **hazing,** defined by www.hazingprevention.org as "any action taken or any situation created intentionally that causes embarrassment, harassment, or ridicule and risks emotional and/or physical harm to members of a group or team" (Hazing, 2021). Examples of hazing include:

- Forced activities for new recruits to "prove" their worth to join
- Required consumption of alcohol

- Humiliation of new or potential members
- Isolation of new or potential members
- Beatings, paddling, or other physical acts against new or potential members

Hazing is an example of intense relational aggression, where the social capital of joining an organization that brings prestige and professional connections and employs power differentials to enforce painful procedures, can become increasingly toxic. This is not directed at Greek life in general, and in fact, they can serve as an affinity group for those that seek them out, as there's no harm in a group of friends organized for a single cause. The blame is on fraternal organizations like Tim Piazza's that allowed prior events to occur with similar outcomes, only this time, Piazza's pain was permanent, as would be the punishment for their fraternity as a whole.

I talked with Kaitlyn about the whole affair, CBS, *USA Today*, and other local news networks scouring every source of the story. I reached out to Tim Piazza's parents, and watched as they pushed to pass antihazing laws and created the Timothy J. Piazza Memorial Foundation and donate over fifty thousand dollars to children's prosthetics.

"It can happen to anyone," said Tim's father, Jim Piazza. "If it was anyone else in his shoes that night, Tim would've carried them to the hospital."

"It starts off slow," he warned. "These cycles of abuse start off with just one thing, one dare, one ask, and then they escalate to the point where what happens to my son happens to someone else. It just takes one. *Be a social disruptor if you have to; don't let the bad things happen when you can do something good.*"

College is a transition period, from high school and late teens to professionalism and early adulthood. You will learn a lot, and still be learning more, as you graduate. Social capital can be an incredibly positive force that creates affinity groups and opens up opportunities that are not normally there for others, but we must also be aware of the toxic side of power over people. Peer pressure and groupthink can cause damage, in school and beyond, and so learning how to disrupt that is a crucial skill to develop in this time.

To make the most of your moment in college means using the social capital, all this knowledge you've acquired, to do some good. But how? I spoke with three class presidents to find what they had in common, and what you can learn to use social capital to be a student leader on campus.

HOW TO BE A STUDENT
LEADER ON CAMPUS

As someone who'd never served as even a class president for high school, the idea of student leaders fascinates me, and I wanted some perspective on what it takes to be one. I compiled some questions, gathered some people, and found out just what it takes to make a difference on campus.

Enter Donovan, Devin, and Morgan, three class presidents at my undergraduate institution.

How do you define a student leader?

"I think a student leader can be defined in many ways. However, I don't think that your grades are one of them. Yes, there are some traits that seem to fit both strong leaders and strong students. Speaking from personal experience, corporate finance was [a] very difficult course for me, but it certainly didn't hold me back from being a student leader—if anything it taught me that everyone has their weaknesses. Ultimately, being involved within the campus community allows you to find people and organizations you share interests with."

DEVIN ROSSI

Donovan agreed, advising hopeful presidential candidates to be ambitious go-getters and to not shy away from opportunities when presented. He made goals, set out to achieve them, and was ready to make some sacrifices with free time, hard choices, and no-win situations with the mindset of helping the most amount of people.

"I believe that all student leaders on campus have one thing in common: They are all so dedicated. Whether students are leaders in Greek life, athletics, or SGA, Susquehanna student leaders are unmatched in their level of dedication. I believe that a good leader does not strive to do every task and activity possible, but is so dedicated to the tasks that they do take on that those tasks are completed successfully."

MORGAN DUBBS

But let's back up a little bit; who are these former class presidents? And how did they get where they are (and how can we replicate their success)?

"I began my SGA as a class representative, the lowest-ranking class officer position. The following year I was planning to run for class president, but former SGA President Christina Martin reached out to me and encouraged me to run for an executive officer position and the rest is history!"

MORGAN DUBBS

Morgan describes her experience with the Community Clean Sweep program as what kept her going toward the presidency. Devin tells a similar story:

"During my time at Susquehanna I found my love of leadership in multiple areas of campus. Upon joining orientation team I started as an orientation leader, which I loved, that propelled me to continue on to lead staff where I ultimately served as the orientation coordinator going into my senior year. I was able to hold an executive board position in my sorority, Alpha Delta Pi, where I served as the vice president of events management. My biggest leadership position was and continues to be my role as the class of 2020 president."

DEVIN ROSSI

On how she managed all these differing roles, she cites effective communication with those you work with, capitalizing on everyone's strengths and building a strong team that meets and exceeds expectations. Resilience is a trait that should be carried throughout life, but when it comes to being a student leader you must remind yourself you are stronger than the circumstances you currently endure, and you are capable of handling these matters gracefully, even as you navigate them yourself.

Donovan links his cultural background, familial upbringing, and strive toward social justice as the biggest indicators he'd be heavily involved on campus.

"As a student of color in a predominantly white institution, it is quite a different experience than one would initially expect. However, it does come with some advantages. It gives you connectivity and a sense of community with all the other students of color on

campus. That community is important because it allows me to be true to myself and to my people."

What's one piece of advice you'd give to this incoming class you wished had been given to you?

Morgan: *"My advice to other students would be: Never think you're not qualified for a position. If you want something, go for it! You never know what opportunities will come your way if you just put yourself out there; first-year students, delve into the college experience! It's ok to switch majors, change friend groups, and try out many different activities. No two college experiences will look alike so own yours and make it your own!"*

Donovan: *It certainly was not easy but in order to manage all of my positions I used upwards of four different calendars to track dates and events throughout different organizations. I also had to make sure that I was delegating work and trusting my teammates so that responsibilities would be taken care of.*

Devin: *The uncharted territories may test you but the tools that you have at your disposal, whether it be something you hold within yourself or the support of your team—those are the things that will keep you grounded in times like this. While each of these positions were different, there is one common denominator that helped me get there: passion. I found my passion for helping to create positive student experiences whether it was for a first year or senior; I searched for ways that I could fulfill that goal and these positions* *allowed me to do that.* **Find your passion and then take opportunities that best align you with that goal.** *Soon enough you'll find like-minded people who will continue to introduce you to new ways to fuel your passion—you never know, maybe it'll turn into a career.*

Social capital can be difficult to acquire, but not impossible. It's more than just soft skills and sweet-talking, but about establishing firm relationships you can both benefit from and enjoy being a part of. And remember, social capital can be as small or as large as you require. In a class and forgot the homework? The classmate you barely talk to might help you out by lending you a pencil. As an RA, please do reach out to us, as even we can be your Campus Champions. One of my closest friends today was someone I served as an RA for, and he has said it made all the difference with adjusting to a new environment knowing I was there for him. How do you do so?

- *Not every opportunity is organized*, so take advantage of the natural moments that build a relationship. Organized workshops are great but so too are the unstructured events that occur every day. Meeting in a lunchroom, in a coffee shop, or passing by in the halls are also ways to form meaningful connections.
- *Trust takes time,* so be sure to give yourself some breathing room. Not every relationship clicks neatly on the first try, and taking the time to form those strong bonds is equally important.

Acquiring social capital is key in cultivating trust, building strong relationships, and pursuing future endeavors, though we must all be willing to be social disruptors whenever and wherever we see it.

"So, that's your origin story, huh? That's why you say what you say and do what you do?" Annalise asked.

"Something like that."

"Well, I like it. That's sweet. You oughta write a book."

"Or start a blog."

"Or a YouTube channel. That'll be the day."

"No, seriously!" she said. "You should. You're always talking about helping others; why not put your money where your mouth is? Call it, I don't know, *First-Generation... College Student... Study Guide.*"

"...or we don't call it that," I told her. "Try something a little classier, yeah? Like, maybe, *First Gen Class.* Yeah, there ya go. Have some fanciness to it, gets the point across. I mean I'd have to check if the domain name was open and then look into search engine optimization..."

"Heh. Nerd talk. Nerdy but cute. Look at you, taking care of everybody and their mother—literally, in your case. I'm just peeling back the layers on you, Mr. Fenstermacher."

"Uh-huh. And when do we peel back the layers on you?"

"Maybe another night, think I'm getting another lockout call. That... and I'm dead-tired." She laughed.

"Yeah, I'm pretty beat myself. Sterling's roped me into another thing tomorrow. Guy really wants me to join his fraternity. Don't know much about them, but I'll let you know how it all goes."

"You better. And it'd be a lot easier if we weren't both stuck in our dorms all weekend. Not that I don't like breaking up a loud party at 3:00 a.m. but..."

"Could be doing other things. Like sleeping."

"Exactly. My hall's super loud, always partying. How'd you get so lucky? I wish I was over there with you."

"I wish you were too." And the words were out of my mouth, a deeper meaning jumping out with them and through the line, though if she heard it, she didn't let on. "We could talk without super weird static breaking up our convos. We could... well, you know."

And now it's unmistakable, the same deeper meaning sending an involuntary chill down my spine and sparking up the heart again, a pulse pounding I'm sure she can hear on her end.

"Oh really?" I said with a smile. "And what exactly would we do?"

"Well... let me tell you."

3

CULTURAL
CURRENCY CREATES
OPPORTUNITY

HOW TO MAKE
MORE MONEY

———

"If you think education is expensive, try ignorance."
DEREK BOK, HARVARD UNIVERSITY PRESIDENT

Well, I was definitely building some social capital with Annalise.

But while I started talking with her, I also had to talk money with myself, and my lack of it. Taking a girl on a date might cost a pretty penny (and she was worth it!) but I had other bills to pay—cell phone, car insurance, books for the new semester, and any other act of God that could wrack up some debt. There's no easy solution: I got to work. I mean, nose to the grindstone, roll-up-your-sleeves-and-dig-in type of work, and the paydays made it all worth it. See, by this point, I think I've hammered home the fact I'm not made of money, so when I tell you I made one thousand dollars in two weeks, there's no gimmicks, just a game plan getting some great returns. This is the kind of money-making-and-managing mentorship I wish I had a few years back.

HOW TO MAKE MORE MONEY

It's simple, but not easy: **Create multiple flows of income**, one active and passive, and if your college allows, one in-class income. Sure, you could log a gazillion hours from a gazillion jobs while living in the No Fun Zone for four years, but that's cheating a little. My aim is to maximize your time, which is money, in order to make the most out your earnings per working period.

My undergraduate campus, like others, has a limit on how many hours students can work. For example: twenty hours weekly, with a forty-hour cap for a two-week period. Let's say you're paid minimum wage ($7.25), and exceed that limit; now we're talking overtime, where an institution may pay up to 1.5 times the regular hourly rate in hours excess to forty. Go to a school where yearly raises are in order, and you're adding up to fifty cents annually. Sounds small, but adds up when by senior year you make $1.50 more at *each* of your jobs. Include promotions, which can be a whole dollar more, and you can possibly earn $8.50 an hour as a sophomore.

My aim isn't to give you a math lesson or economics lecture; I'm showing you how my time management model allowed for an ample social life, and I still didn't have to worry about putting gas in the car. Speaking of, if you work on campus, you won't need to worry as much about that mileage to work if you're a block away!

WHY WORK ON CAMPUS?

On-campus employment benefits you by being close to where you live, study, and eat, as well as usually being willing to work with your academic schedule. Off-campus employers might not understand the ins and outs of the school/work tug and pull, while working at the campus library you've spent hours studying at has people aware of why you might be a few minutes late clocking in.

Just ask rising Susquehanna University senior Kristen Blair how she does it. Kristen's both a building manager and award-winning thrower for the college track team, carving out time for her sports and studies.

"I have practice about ten hours during the week, then a full day's worth of a [track] meet, then having to go to work the day after getting home late... but I have learned to cope with it... [this] provides me with the skills I will need for time management... it's possible [to earn one thousand dollars] if you're willing to work when you can. To add to that, there are also jobs on campus that give $0.25 or $0.50 raise with each year that you've been working at that job."

KRISTEN BLAIR, SUSQUEHANNA UNIVERSITY STUDENT

Career and job search site www.careerprofiles.com offers college students a practical plan toward maximizing your investments with some dos and don'ts when going for prized positions.

ACING THE INTERVIEW
- **Don't ask what you should already know.** This one's simple. Walk in with some prior knowledge on the company and what they do, and have some general questions ready for after your interview to show your engagement with the job description that showcases your aptitude and willingness to put time and effort in. As someone who's been on both sides of an interview desk, one immediate spot of contention for candidates is when they show a lack of

knowledge on the basic items of interest concerning their position. If you're looking for a job in the medical or technology center, some basic terminology should be familiar to you, as well as the outline of the job requirements.

- **Do have a conversation, not an interrogation.** Relax! This isn't as one sided as you think, and you are here to feel out the organization as much as they are looking to find a capable, compatible candidate for the position. Going along with the advice above, don't be so overprepared that you are unable to show some humanity and personality during this job search. After all, interviewers want someone with the hard skills to get the job done, as well as the soft skills to add to the workplace culture and collaborate well with others. Showing that sparkly, smiley personality will go a long way towards that.

- **Don't be negative**. This is a big one, especially if you had an adversarial experience with your previous employer or coworkers. A common question asked concerns conflict resolution or how you handled a stressful situation in the past. Not only does this test your interpersonal and problem-solving skills toward a scenario, but also your attitude toward them. Remaining positive, or, if that's near impossible, neutral, toward times you'd rather not remember, can demonstrate your professionalism and resilience in the face of complications—traits that certainly have positive rapport with interviewers.

- **Do stay on topic.** Keep the focus on relevant subject matter. This is the key component to strategic storytelling, and I'd advise starting each story you tell with a beginning, middle, and end in mind. Your start must be a qualified hook for listeners, the middle is where you actively solve the problem, and the end is to keep you from just trailing off. I've been through so many interviews where a captivating story tapers off with no real conclusion, dampening its impact. Transferable experiences are great for star storytelling, allowing you to bookend your story with the lesson learned and the strength you gained from the interaction. Have your high-impact examples on hand for when you go to an interview!

In fact, being a scrappy student can make all the difference in acing an interview. I've compiled **five zero-skill ways to succeed at job searching.**

1. Don't be late.
2. Bring extra resumes/bodies of your work.
3. Ask a question to demonstrate interest.
4. Be polite.
5. Be passionate about the work you do!

All of this should help prepare you in advance, but once you get in there, you're going to face some pretty tough questions, including, but not limited to:

- *What is your greatest weakness?*
- *Why should we hire you?*
- *How do you handle conflict with a coworker?*

When discussing your greatest weakness, you know that one's often paired with greatest strength, and that both are a staple of this process and should be expected as a given. You don't want to humble brag about your greatest strength or overemphasize your greatest weakness. The solution is to employ strategic vulnerability and objective strength.

Strategic vulnerability refers to actual pain points you have, so none of that "I am just too dedicated to my work!" here. You should be honest, but not give the impression you shouldn't be hired because of it. For me, I admit I had a hard time with the math section of the standardized test given every year. I inform them that, knowing this weak spot, I've since taken on added responsibilities to test and grow those skills. The same guy that could barely solve those math problems was now assessing the SEO (search engine optimization) strategies, calculating professionals' payrolls, and triangulating the data analytics for the podcast I served as assistant producer for.

Objective strength takes out any subjectivity to your exploits, stating the facts that helped attain the end result and how they can be repeated in the job you're going for. This way, you're not hyping yourself up, just stating the skills that solved a task at hand, and how those transferable skills can be useful in the position you're applying for.

Once you've aced that interview and are settling in at an on-campus job, why not diversify those income sources and start getting the best bang for your buck? Here's how.

THE KINDS OF INCOME
TO CASH IN BIG

YOUR PASSIVE INCOME

You've probably heard of work-study programs* offering paid positions, where you make money while having the time to finish schoolwork. The flexible hours and "*hold down the fort*" mentality make it ideal for working another job in the same time frame. Think library assistant, arts gallery attendant, or front desk manager. If no one's stopping by the desk, time to make some extra cash!

*NOTE: *Becoming a residential assistant, depending on the university, will either be a paid position or possibly cover room and board with a meal plan alternative offered to you. Full disclosure as an RA, this is something you should do!*

YOUR ACTIVE INCOME

Next, seek out an "active" campus position like online tutoring or social media manager. You'll find these positions often require returning phone calls, answering emails, or proofreading papers online. The takeaway here is that they are all easy to pick up/put down at a moment's notice, which is bound to happen at some point during one of your passive income jobs.

YOUR IN-CLASS INCOME

You won't find this category in any business textbooks, but I'm sure you'd like to earn cash while earning your degree. Many universities (like mine, thankfully) offer in-class note takers, where the notes you take for a class are now a paid endeavor! If notes are needed for a class, you'll be notified and can vie for the position, logging the hours you've taken notes for in class. Nice to get paid for something you should probably be doing already, to be honest. Check with your university's academic tutoring department for open positions.

TYING IT ALL TOGETHER

Feel free to get creative! Take a semester easy and apply for more passive jobs to catch up on schoolwork, or dedicate yourself to clocking more hours in for your active income position. There are laws for how many hours a student can work biweekly, with only so much overtime, and work-study can run out eventually. In fact, here are the top tips to saving money while in college.

- Spend less than you earn: Make a budget and stick to it. When you have an excess or surplus of money on a monthly basis, be sure to save that for a rainy day. Treat savings like a priority, because they will be in an emergency.
- Stick to savings goals: By making a game or competition with yourself out of it, you hold yourself accountable for staying on point.
- Build good credit, not credit card debt: Your credit score will follow you all your life, so setting yourself up for success rather than failure is essential. Failing to plan is

planning to fail. Having a credit card you pay off incrementally by making payments on time is an easy way to do this while having a job on campus. You're learning a lot more than just learning at school, you see.

- Prioritize interest-only payments: Do you know how much the average college loan debt is per student? Approximately $32,000. Let's just say that's yours too; it'll be much more by the time you get to it. Yes, you will have a six months grace period to find a job and settle in, but you're not just paying back the thirty-two thousand dollars, you're also paying a little thing called *interest,* which will grow with you for however long the debt remains unpaid.

Student loan company found online at www.credible.com averages the typical compound interest, the rate you pay over time with your student loan, at around 4–7 percent. To find out yours specifically is simple:

[Loan Amount] X [Interest Rate] and then determine spread that out over [Loan Term], which is just how many years you'll be paying it. All of this will help you build credit, have money, and collect savings while you're in college, and since you're budgeting well, you can even enjoy life a little with what you have left over after necessities.

Don't expect, I repeat, *don't* expect two things:

1. That you'll make one thousand dollars first thing as a first year and
2. That this is the be all, end all of get-rich-quick scheme.

To make that much in such a short time span is *possible,* but not always *plausible.* Covering people's shifts constantly and never missing any of your own *could* result in something similar, but again, time is money. Now more so than ever we are aware of how our mental states can affect our work performance and personal relationships. "Doubling hours" can help you earn more in a shorter amount of time with your in-class income adding to that and leaving the rest open for you to prioritize your academics and enjoy what some call the best four years of your life.

Remember that you're at (*insert college name here*) for an education, first and foremost, and that having downtime for yourself is not a bad thing. Money will be talking later, too. College is a time for expanding your mindset and having new experiences, and as we've pointed out before, can be the most or least diverse area for a whole class of students. While counting up all your coins and cash, be sure to collect **cultural currency** as well. Study.com defines cultural currency as the assets to give us social mobility.

Sounds a lot like social capital, right? Let me explain the difference.

Social capital is like the social connections you make with others, while cultural currency refers to the knowledge of norms and values, in our case, referring to college. Social capital can *get* you to college; cultural currency is what you develop as you *ingratiate* yourself into the institution, as I definitely had been at that time. I was in admissions, making money, got the girl, and joined the fraternity with Sterling. Things were looking up. I had high social capital and was just now starting to develop cultural currency by understanding my **school climate and culture.**

The National School Climate Center defines climate as "major spheres of school life such as safety, relationships, teaching and learning, and the environment as well as larger organizational patterns," while school culture refers to the "personality" of the school itself (Education Solutions, 2020). Are most students friendly, and walk about in large groups, or do they tend to walk alone, buried in their phones, with not a lot of space for outdoor recreation? My small liberal arts school was famous for its wide-open green lots for pick-up games of ultimate frisbee and flag football, and on a sunny day, you'd have a hard time not tripping over people in lawn chairs. People would look up and smile at you, wishing you well and waving away. It was definitely a friendly campus, though when I'd visit friends in their city-based schools, the assumption was you'd walk from point A to B, with no dallying in between.

But what do all these differing expectations have to do with prepping you for higher education?

For so many students of color, we tend to "white-wash" our resumes and experiences—that is, to remove any mention of our racial identity from the list of accomplishments we share so as to better our chances of getting hired. The Harvard Business School found removing details pertaining to race resulted in a 15 percent increase in callbacks from companies. Harvard professor Anthony Abraham Jack wrote a whole book on this called *The Privileged Poor: How Elite Colleges Are Failing Disadvantaged Students*. His studies identified "privileged poor," minority students who served as *model* minority students from prep schools with the well-off parents, and the "doubly-disadvantaged," the underserved students from under-resourced schools. In his TED talk, he says:

> *We have paid less attention to what happens when students get on campus than their means of entry and where they go once they graduate.*
>
> ANTHONY ABRAHAM JACK

As much as we hope it's all clear skies and rainbows once you step on campus, the reality is, it just might not be. A lot of underrepresented students step onto schools where they're the only ones that look like them, speak the same language, or understand the cultural norms that remind them of home. Website Viking Fusion cites a Hap.org report that found at least 30 percent of college students experience some form of homesickness. Seventy percent of first years were slated to go through severe homesickness. In this sense, accumulating cultural currency, or understanding how your college operates and how you'd thrive while there, is just as important as the financial capital it takes to go there at all.

The path for progress is different for everyone and being aware of where we are is important to keep progressing. Dr. Towuanna Porter-Brannon, president at Thomas Nelson Community College, builds upon this premise with advice of her own during our interview:

I've had exposure to other experiences, to Black excellence, to the extremities that can be found at a PWI (predominantly white institution). In our efforts, we must not bend to tribalism. It is not simply, 'You can trust anyone who looks like you; distrust anyone who doesn't.' Us underrepresented students already struggle with our self-efficacy, and so hearing, 'You have to work twice as hard to get half as far,' only doubles the doubt we have for ourselves. Do the best you can, be the best you, and stay focused on you while at college. The world needs more of you, and there'll be enough people already in your way, so stand get in there too.

DR. PORTER BRANNON

As you might've guessed, there's a story for that too.

This is the story of cultures clashing, Greek life on life support, and how our cultural differences can help define our defining years on campus.

CULTURE SHOCK

My second year on campus was only the first year I'd been part of a Greek organization, with house rules and all. And it'd all gone swimmingly until now. See, besides Sterling and I, only about five other members of color were a part of the club, and tensions across race lines were beginning to show and crack. Or I should say, they became more apparent. There'd been some mumbling, disgruntled talk before about the lack of diversity and improper inclusive activities, well intentioned, but well beside the point.

This time, however, intentions aside, the impact was deafening, and the reverberations would be felt across the collegiate landscape. A group text conversation open only to fraternity members was friendly enough, a few jabs here, random updates there, and maybe a meme or two when someone found them funny enough to be shared. What was not common was the use of racial epithets in casual conversation. A *bleep* from the phone and a push of a button later, and I'm beside myself at the brazen obscenity on screen.

The N-Word. Hard R.

I always wonder why we use euphemisms like this, like describing it as the "N" versus the "C" and "F" word is any better when it just conjures the word in our minds. So too was the rightful anger roused in the chat, a series of expletives symbolizing surprise, disdain, and distaste.

"Sorry!" Damon, the one who sent the message said. "Wrong chat!"

Wrong chat. Not, *I'm sorry, I shouldn't have used that word* or *I'm so, so, sorry, I don't know how that happened?* Just, *wrong chat*. It didn't sit well with me, and even after the inciting incident was deleted, it was not from the memories of the members involved. Many of us, but not Damon, were at a charity event for the organization, and so in the field house we all gathered to gripe about this most recent grievance.

"Just can't believe that actually happened. Like, here. To us! This is central PA, not the freaking Deep South!" said an underclassman.

"Get real. You're surprised? Turn on the news channel and maybe realize we're not in some post-racial paradise. Cops kill us, the news hate us, and we gotta deal with... *people* like him who toss around that word like it don't mean what it means," an upperclassman said.

"Forget all that, what're we gonna do about it? Like you said, world's gettin' crazier every day. We're gettin' shot up and no one's doin' nothin' about it. Time to do *somethin'*, I dunno what, I don't care what, but somethin'," a third brother chimed in.

"Yeah," I said, jumping into the conversation. "We should probably take it up with leadership, right? Maybe go to the president, see what he has to say about all this? We could even launch a formal complaint."

"BS, man. They don't care. Never have, never will. Tried it before, failed it before. They'll just brush it off like always," said the same upperclassman with experience.

"Look, we can escalate, if need be, but we have to go through the proper channels first, you know? Cover our backsides, then put 'em on blast, right? C'mon," I reasoned. "We go in guns-a'-blazin', and we're sure to get nicked in the crossfire."

"Apt word of choice," said a familiar voice, and our huddled group parted to make room for another clever member. Sterling, strained and under stress, stalked over like a big cat with claws on full display. "Black. Lives. Matter. Our lives matter, and you're all over here tryin' to break bread with *them?* Nah. Not this time. This time, we let 'em know who they can and can't mess with."

An uncomfortable awe falls over the assembled, eyes not meeting his gaze and feet nervously twisting in place. He takes time to look for eyes that meet his, fails, and snorts in disgust.

"We need a show of force. Like you said, man. Somethin', I dunno, something big. Somethin' that leaves a lasting impression, that we can build our case on."

"Like... like a brick?" All eyes turn to the greenest of newbies, a small Brown boy with big round glasses and tiny wrists that he massages nervously.

"Maybe... maybe we put a brick through the window at the Big House? N-Nobody'd get hurt, but I know it'd sure scare me." We all stare in astonishment. "I saw it on TV. Some protesters were doing it. They were saying, 'Property versus person damage, whattya you prefer?' So I thought... maybe we could try that?"

I wait for an inevitable full stop, the heat of the moment cooling over at the realization this young kid, barely out of his momma's home, is suggesting vandalism to our own home.

It never comes.

"Lil' man with the big plan over here!" And a clap on the back.

"Who'd have thought the new kid would bring up some old-school justice!" And a fist bump.

The only one who looks hesitant is Sterling, with a thoughtful expression as he ponders the proposition. He's hotheaded, sure, but still wants his attached by this thing's end.

"We do that and we're done. We're caught and we're outta the org, off of campus for sure. That's a crime, and another brother in jail ain't helpin' anybody."

"So we don't do it, then. I got some buddies in Black Student Union. They'll toss the brick, and we'll be none the wiser!" said the upperclassman, and by God, I thought I saw Sterling consider it, a king not looking to be outdone in his own court.

"And if there was another way?" I interjected. "A more peaceful path, then what? We don't take it? I say we expend all options first, turn over every stone and then, if we can't find an answer then..." Sterling smiled sinfully.

"We toss that stone through their freaking window."

CULTURE CLASH

———

I knew change needed to happen fast, lest Sterling's spark set ablaze all the goodwill we'd fostered in our shared organization. So I went to the most functionally literate person I knew on campus: Skye, the president of the Black Student Union.

"I gotta admit, surprised you're here," she said when I set up our chat in the small campus cafe. "But I'm glad ya did. Honest. This *really* doesn't look good for y'all," she said.

"No, it doesn't. But there's some talks of violence, and I'm trying to mitigate damage. Be the difference and all, you know?"

"Y'all ever think maybe they deserve what's comin' to 'em? Whatever it is, it's not like their record's ever been too clean. And now they're dropping the N-word? Hard-R? Maybe sit this fight out, champ. Let someone else do the punching up for a change."

"Maybe they don't deserve our help, but I can't not do something when everyone else does nothing. And what they're planning is a punishable offense. A brick through a window. What'll that get you?" I asked.

"Justice," she answered.

"No, it'll get you unpaid time off from school permanently, along with a permanent record. And if they're talking like someone from your org's gonna do it, even if they don't, that can implicate a lot of people, including you. Look, I know Damon's not the best—"

"Hol' up. *Damon* did this?"

Damon, the blond-haired, blue-eyed boy with a big smile and even bigger mouth, was as bombastic as he was bubbly—bulb so bright it might hurt your eyes. Parties were a popular pastime of his, and Skye was no stranger to them either. It's not impossible to believe they could've crossed paths. Perhaps due to my own biases blinding me, I somehow thought them worlds apart, far beyond the other's support. And yet, she seemed to know him, eyes widening as mouth hung open, agape. Before, Skye set a snarky, sarcastic smile on display, now replaced by a worrisome look that wore down her usual defenses. A national conversation just got some personal stakes.

"He didn't. No way he did it," she said.

"He did," I answered.

"No. No, you shut up. Just shut up a sec. I-I know him. He's a good kid, means well, this whole thing's just... it's just gone out of control."

"You don't say."

"...We can fix this. Yeah, it's just where he's from. You said he meant it for the other chat, right? He shouldn't have said it, yeah, I get it, but let's not ruin his life over it."

"I agree. I'm here to offer a nonlethal approach to our mutual problem. You've got BSU's support; I've got an in with the fraternity. I write these web articles, yeah?" She rolled her eyes. "They can help us. We get the truth out before this becomes a worse PR mess than it is. You know this campus; it's way too small and everyone knows everyone and everything. We wait, and we'll be on the defensive, we'll be playing cleanup after the damage's been done. He'll tell his side of the story, heck, we can even get our president and faculty adviser to sign off on it. We'll have 'em pledge to do better, have some diversity training, and make a learning experience out of it."

Is it any wonder I would switch majors from creative writing to public relations?

"They damn well better," Skye said, though her voice, shaky and cracking, did not match the steely gaze she tried to keep with water brimming at its sides.

"Hey, c'mon. We got this, yeah? You and me. Us. We're doing the right thing here," she took a deep breath.

"You really think so?"

"I do," I said.

I hope, I thought.

Skye set up the meet with Damon, our sidebar at the local watering hole in town. Most townsfolk there were well into their forties, folks just getting off from work and the usual crowd all exchanging pleasantries, the humdrum of the day-to-day blocking out of conversation. Here, we talked through all the details of Damon's story, his version of events he recounted while anxiously peering over our shoulders the entire time.

"I know I was wrong, okay? I know I was. And I'm sorry. Really sorry! I'm not racist, I swear. It just, like, slipped out or something," he explained, but since I was the one telling this story, I was forced to press for more.

"It 'slipped out' when typing a text message to friends?" I asked politely.

"Yes! I mean, no, well... look, I didn't say it to anybody Black. Back home, that word just means, like, 'stupid' or 'weird' or whatever."

"Then why don't you just say that?" I replied. "Why specifically use a word you know would cause problems. You knew the second you sent that message, didn't you? That's why you deleted it so quickly."

"I don't know! I should've, alright, I get that. It's just, like, hard, when you're talkin' to folks back home and ya fall back into that old way of talking. My friends back home don't get this stuff, man. They don't know any better."

And it seems you don't quite get it either, I pondered.

"But I understand you all gotta do what you gotta do. I effed up and now there's gotta be consequences. Hold me accountable and all that."

"Damon, listen. We're trying to make this a learning experience for everyone here," I said, and Skye sat her hand on his in support. "What you did, not gonna lie, man, that shook some people up, and not in a good way. But you know that. I'm more 'educate the hate' than 'show your *fists* to ra*cists*.'"

"I'm not—"

"I know, I know. Bad joke. Figure of speech. But if you give the okay that this is how you want your words to appear in text..."

And he does. And we left, all going our separate ways. Skye hung back a bit, whispered something in his ear, and with a hug she was down the road making her way back to campus a few blocks down the cobblestone road. Damon thanked me for everything, waved, and hopped back in his parents' shiny silver car. Me? I headed back to the Big House, and ready my statement to the president and faculty adviser. Once that was done, I sent this to the world wide web for the whole world to see... or at least, on campus, which can feel like the whole wide world in the moment.

Once the web article starting circulating, this small liberal arts campus became a hot spot for scandalous school speech, Greeks gossiping to Greeks, sports players swapping stories, a whispering campaign that wandered through our little world. As I ambled across campus, I was met with as many claps on the shoulder as I was given cold ones, made as many new friends as it seemed I did enemies. Many felt like this was finally a mark on the unblemished organization, who in turn were pretty satisfied with how things turned out. After all, it could have been much worse.

Some thought we didn't go far enough.

I relayed all this to Annalise the next night, the two of us splayed across the couch in her residence hall, two friends far too close to even call it that.

"I mean, I'm in the right, right?" I asked.

"Right," she replied cheekily.

"No, seriously. Like, in the grand scheme of things, are we in the right? Is what I'm doing, you know, *good?* Think Damon's looking to drop from the org. Last I heard, he was talking to the president and things weren't looking too good. They're saying it's all mutual, but I don't know. And the org president said he wants me on some special council so I guess there's some upside, but still." She sighed and sat up. "What?"

"I almost don't wanna tell you."

"No, tell me. C'mon. I'll beg."

"Alright, but don't, like, freak out or anything." She turned to face me. "Damon's done. He got fired. Well, he got fired from one job here on campus, and then the other called him up asking if what they heard was true... and then *they* fired him. It's his last year, though, so he's just gotta last till graduation, but he is *persona non grata* 'round these parts."

"And that is all on account of me." I rolled back and face palmed with both hands. "Great. Where's my award. Worst Person Ever. I know it was a tight race between the candidates, but I feel I really stepped up my game from last year."

"Stop it, Noah. You know you're not *that* bad of a person." I jokingly glared at her.

"Look, college isn't about getting it perfect, right? It's about... the process, figuring this all out, making mistakes, getting better, and then looking back at how stupid you were," she flashed me a toothy grin. "And hey, it wasn't that stupid, if you ask me. You did what you thought was best, which is all any of us can do. Made a sucky situation... less sucky, and yeah, Damon got a little roughed up, but he's only got a few weeks left in the year till he's graduated. You? You've got two whole years left ahead of ya. So lighten up a little, will ya?" She edged herself closer to me on the couch. "For me?"

Yeah, she had the effect on me, and I edged closer to her myself.

"Yeah, maybe for you. Maybe," I said with a smile, and playfully pushed her back onto her side with a laugh, then see the notifications on my phone go off.

And continued to go off.

By the time I've got my phone out of my pocket, a whopping twelve seconds later, there's nearly double that in social media activity concerning me, and it's not good. For those unaware, there's a phenomenon known as 'subtweeting,' typically referring to Twitter (hence the name) but spanning to all social networks, where one makes posts about specific individuals without naming them. Examples are:

That moment the racist in your org calls everyone else racist.

@ everyone who can't take a joke: lighten up or eff off!

When underclassmen think they know better than their uppers... smh (shaking my head).

This is kind of hard to miss when you're all in the same circles. Annalise peeked over my shoulder and could see slew of online libel. She rubbed my back sympathetically. "No good deed, huh?"

"No good deed, indeed." Then I shot up. "But I'm not just sitting back and taking this. I mean, who am I to do that? I've dealt with this before..."

"And when you do the things you do and say the things you say..."

"You can't be surprised to face the things you face. As usual, you're right," I said. "But don't go letting it inflate your head. That thing's big enough already." She had the expected mouth agape and her eyes widened, and I let out a laugh that brought back the confidence of yesteryear; I would get through this.

And get through to them, hopefully.

HOW YOU CAN COLLECT CULTURAL CURRENCY... STARTING RIGHT NOW!

We met every Sunday, all eighty fraternity members.

We're in a spacious seminar hall that doubled as a theater and had the acoustics to accompany it—all eighty rowdy, refined, respectful, riled-up record breakers of campus leadership that served on nearly every board, approving every motion passed. As Sterling would say, you didn't make a move without their majority rule, and when a majority of that voting power was in the very room, you wanted to stay on their good side. You did not walk in there ready to give a speech on all that they'd done wrong, tell them they were not above reproach, and then proceed to walk out unscathed.

But I did.

I went in there, asked for a moment to speak during general assembly of items to be addressed, and was handed a microphone at the front of the stage, podium and all. In hindsight, maybe I should've brought notes? Nah, this was from the heart, honest and true, and I wouldn't change a thing.

"I'd like to explain myself," I started. "There's been a lot of behind-the-scenes activity going on here, and based on your social media profiles, we're all a bit worried. I get that. I also want to straighten out the record because I believed we were upstanding gentlemen, that when we had something to say, we said it to each other's faces because we had at least that common decency for one another. Maybe I was wrong, but I don't think I am.

"I think tensions are high right now. In the country, on campus, in our club. And I think it'll get easier, it will, but only after we've confronted this conflict that's splintered us for so long." I spied Damon in the upper seating area, hunched over as shoulders rocked to the tune of silent sobs, and it nearly broke me to see him like this.

"What happened... what happened was a mistake. A costly one, but one that I hope we can all learn from. I don't think any one individual here is intentionally, purposefully racist. I don't believe this org is. What I do believe is that we have the power to make a difference, all of us right here in this room, and that is why I said what I said. I wanted to bring us closer together, to ensure what got out wasn't something twisted. Case in point, look how many of you thought I was out to hurt the org, when I was only trying to help it." Some nodded and some faces that were constricted in contempt relaxed as I went on.

"And I know there are questions. In the interest of being honest, and fair, I'd like to take this time to answer any and all questions you might have, so when we leave, we leave here just a little more united."

And they did.

From as far back as I could remember, I was the "whitest-sounding Black kid," an epithet I couldn't escape no matter how hard I tried. Talk "Black"? What did that even mean? Were they referring to African American Vernacular English (AAVE), better known as slang? Not everyone that looked like me talked like that, but then again, maybe they'd never talked to someone who looked like me *other* than me. They lacked the cultural currency to understand any walk of life beyond their own, and for the longest time, their only reprimand was an awkward interaction or two.

According to the United Fund, a philanthropy donating to Black student scholarships, 57 percent of Black high school students will have the correct math and science courses to be ready for the college level (Bridges, 2020).

According to collegiate advice site What To Become, English is not the first language of 20 percent of first-generation students (Jacimovic, 2020).

And more than 60 percent of American college students have experienced food insecurity according to AAC&U News (Dedman, 2019).

...[T]here is a food pantry that the Chaplain set up and we are allowed to use stuff from there. It's great but only when I get a chance to leave and go over there.
REBECCA, SUSQUEHANNA UNIVERSITY CLASS OF 2021

For Rebecca, Susquehanna doubles as both her school and temporary home, providing her with a place to safely stay and food to keep her healthy. I reached out to Kutztown University to speak with their Assistant Director of Annual Giving, Keegan Meyers, a Shikellamy High School graduate like myself, who explained:

I would say that one of the largest misconceptions people have about university education is that the only purpose is to make the university more money than they already have. Honestly, there are so many expenses from a university standpoint, such as <u>emergent student need,</u> that need so much more additional support than alumni and others may realize.

KEEGAN MEYERS

Where college is concerned, its cultural currency is more than meets the eye. Going to college will help you refine two aspects of your cultural capital:

1. **Institutionalized,** the specialized knowledge gained from your degree
2. **Embodied,** the skills you've learnt along the way in your field of interest

The degree will say you know what you are doing, and X University says so, while what you embody is what you have learned along the way. While important to bring in financial income, understanding the way of this new way of life will also be necessary for your adjustment. For me, it was having my blue-collar, lower-income town for a school that some students drove Maserati's to... and their parents and more at home. It meant being the first in my family to go through all the rigors of higher education and having to be a guide for my two younger siblings. By understanding college culture, I better understood how I worked within it, and could help others do the same.

Knowledge isn't power; *applied* knowledge is.

2 TYPES OF CULTURAL CURRENCY TO ACQUIRE

1. **Locate your group's resource center:** For me, I had several questions concerning race on campus, and the Black Student Union provided all the information I needed to feel confident in sharing my story with you. There may also be a women's center, organizations devoted to your religious group, and other affinity memberships. Remember the "How to Use This Book" segment? That list of ten words you might not know can be added to, and it's things like that you'll want a reliable resource for to ensure the proper information is given.

2. **Hone your marketable skills:** This relates back to your getting a degree. We all know it's one of those weed-out questions on job applications. "You must have a bachelor's and X many years' experience." You'll already have the degree, so be sure to find clubs on campus (or start one!) that relate to your major and passion. Developing these will make you invaluable in your area of expertise.

It's a lot, I know. This is a lot. And it's okay for it to *be* a lot sometimes. That's normal. Don't feel you have to be "on" all the time. That's draining and harmful and honestly? Just tiring. It can feel like, especially by this point, you're an imposter on campus trying to "fit in" and like you don't belong. Believe me, by this point, the doubt was creeping up. If I had the experience I do now, I could've seen how burned out us minority students get, and gotten some friends the help they needed.

I could've saved Sterling.

As another example of a cautionary tale, here's exactly why self-care is so critical for your sense of self.

4

YOUR MIND'S THE MUSCLE THAT MATTERS MOST

TACKLING TOXIC POSITIVITY

———

The roots of education are bitter, but the fruit is sweet.

ARISTOTLE

You'll get over it!

Things could be worse!

Just be positive!

While we can't deny the positive impact of optimistic thinking, the refusal to admit or even acknowledge the negative aspects of a situation can prove harmful, especially to college students. Schoolwork, employment, social pressures, and a myriad of other factors weigh us down, and ignoring the fact that we can experience sadness and frustration as well as joy and gratitude is inherently toxic. In fact, it's **toxic positivity.**

Dr. Konstantin Lukin of Psychology Today defines toxic positivity as "keeping positive, and keeping positive only, [believed to be] the right way to live your life. It means only focusing on positive things and rejecting anything that may trigger negative emotions."

How does that relate to the imposter syndrome? What even is it? I sat down with Susquehanna University's Cheryl Stumpf, a therapist at the campus's counseling center, to discuss further. Stumpf, speaking as a therapist, mother of two college kids, and a first-generation graduate herself, had this to say:

> *Imposter syndrome is that feeling like I am portraying someone who knows what they are doing and who they are, when in reality I feel incompetent and afraid of being found out to be a fraud.*
>
> CHERYL STUMPF, MS, NCC, LPC

She went on to describe her own college experience, relating details of the tension between herself and some at home who did not have the same education, and the intense pressure to succeed well and beyond expectations. It's a common story among first-generation students, and one I'm all too familiar with. Kendra Cherry at Verywell Mind lists a few signs someone is suffering from a toxic positivity mindset:

- They exhibit signs of guilt and/or shame for being sad and angry.
- They tend to dismiss or attempt to play off difficult emotional responses, either their own or the reactions of others.
- They apply "quick fixes" like the quotes at the start of this chapter to complex, convoluted problems without any real solutions.

While we can list numerous reasons why this attitude and set of beliefs is inherently harmful, it really boils down to one defining trait: the lack of personal growth, courage to face the things we can, and strength to accept the things we cannot. In fact, by refusing to face our fears, we risk developing imposter syndrome due to the self-doubt digging away at us.

And that's what happened to Sterling.

BAD VIBES ONLY

I'm in the Big House, a country house with more in common with a country club. Crew cuts and crisp, clean candidates all campaign for positions in the executive-level capacity. While most third years claw at any open leadership positions, the main foyer a cluttered mess of networking conversations, I'm sitting back, observing and mulling over recent decisions. I'm done here, that's for certain, the events of last semester leaving a bad taste in my mouth and a bitterness where any sweet ignorance used to be. This isn't the place for me, not the people or the pastimes either, and I could do well off with an extra half a thousand dollars each semester. No offense to anybody that can and will afford it, but there was no way I could or would.

Low lights set the atmosphere of the occasion; palatial pillars of strong oak and a collection of cavernous rooms, halls, and chambers create a classy, archaic scene. Fast-talking, deep-pocketed people put on their fake faces, smiles stuck in place. A single Black dot wades through that wall of white: Sterling. He beelines for me, his arm under mine, and pulls me into a backroom without a word. The crackle of conversation fades with the suddenness of the door, slammed, like being shaken away from a dream. We're in a conference room, a long table splayed out across the middle of the room, the paraphernalia of years long past, parties best forgotten, and a tradition that never will be, line the walls around us as the stained-glass windows overlook a moonlit sky. Sterling locks the door and grasps me by the shoulders.

"What're you doing? You should be out there rubbing elbows, bumping shoulders with these guys, c'mon. The tall one? He's our treasurer, be sure to talk to him. Blond-haired guy? Okay, there's like, ten blondes out there, but the blond wearing the blue tie—" Sterling says, but I cut him off.

"Listen, I'm not playing the game anymore, man. I'm done." He just stares at me, uncomprehending. "I'm done. The fraternity. This... *game* of who knows who: I'm done. I'm leaving the org and, to be honest, I think we both should." He shakes his head vigorously, pacing back and forth and now rubbing his temples while breathing heavily, too deeply, and I start to realize he's not himself.

"No, I don't think we should give up, Noah. I don't think we can all just walk away from this so easily like *you* can. You wanna make a difference, right? Shake things up? Save the world? That means working with the powers that be, keepin' ya head down, and being behind all the right closed doors, not outside 'em. You don't get that yet? That's the way things are."

"I get it. I just don't care," I said. "Let's buck this system. This... this isn't us. We can be, heck, we *are* better than that. We can make moves without their power behind us. I mean, c'mon, you and I are a lot alike, and you know I like to do things my own way."

"So I've noticed," he snaps back.

There's a pause.

"Do we... is something going on, man?" I asked.

"You tell me. I'm just trying to help," he replied. "Isn't that what you say? Right before you screw everything and everyone up?"

"Dude, what's your deal? I thought we were cool, but obviously you've had something to say for a while."

"And when should I have said it? Huh? When you put us all on blast here at the fraternity? When you wrote that post?"

"You were gonna throw a brick through a window!"

"I was not! Some kid said that, I was just, like, talkin' it out. We all threw crazy ideas out there; don't come down on me like it was all my idea. Big, bad Sterling always to blame for everything."

"No one's blaming you; stop it. And I didn't 'put us on blast,' I was doing the best I could for the most amount of people," I said.

"Of course, never 'your' people, just 'people.' Every-freakin'-body. All lives matter, right?" he countered.

"Oh, that is some bull! You know it's not like that so don't even try. I dunno why you're suddenly all up on me, but to be honest, *not* appreciating it."

"All up on ya, huh? 'Dude?' Don't try talkin' Black, man; it ain't your specialty. Shoulda figured that one out at BSU."

"So that's how far back this goes? All the way to year one, *day* one, even? What, is it competition? Are you that threatened by me—"

"By you?"

"—by *me*, that you have to tear someone else down to feel like somebody? Makes a small man outta you, Sterling, I gotta admit."

"Yeah, and whattya you know about it?" he snarled. "Can't ya see? Ain't enough room for two of us, not like I thought. They're fixin' to pit us against one another eventually; why not now? And who're you, really? Some uppity punk ridin' my coattails."

"Didn't realize you were the one that got me to college. Or went to class for me. Yeah, no. That was me. I deserve to be here just as much as you."

"Yeah, and I have *years* on you!" he said in return. "Years of loyalty, and they'd toss that out in a heartbeat for ol' Honest Abe here—you, like you're something special and new."

"Look, I don't see you as competition, man. I thought we were in this together—partners, you and me against the whole lot of 'em... the heck happened, man? Where'd it all go wrong?"

He is heaving now, with labored breaths as he raises a finger, then deflates completely into a chair, nearly missing the edge of the seat with a sob. He lifts his head with what appears to be Herculean effort, and when his eyes reach mine, they're filled to the brim with tears. "What if... we're wrong, man? What if neither of us are 's'posed to be here at all? Just two Black jokes without a punchline? I feel like we're criminals just waiting to be caught. Like we're imposters."

Sterling had imposter syndrome.

HOW TO PROVE (TO YOURSELF) YOU'RE NOT AN IMPOSTER

———

Throughout this whole book, I've tried fighting this.

Writing a college prep book for underrepresented students by an underrepresented student comes with its own challenges. Chief among them is walking the line between helpful and harmful. It's helpful to point out the ways we can circumvent obstacles in our path while remaining realistic about the systemic issues facing us, but harmful if I focus too much on either side of the coin. Place emphasis on the individual, and I risk being seen as going "too easy" on the institution. Pay attention to how much the system is broken, and I risk sounding hopeless and powerless in the face of it all.

And then there's the other big one: the moxie it takes to put pen to paper in the first place! Who am I to write this book? Am I even the best person for the job? I like to think my academic, professional, and personal experience lend credibility, but this vulnerability? This doubt is natural in the minds of many, and by sharing mine with you, I hope you can be honest with yourselves and come to the same conclusion I did: We would not be here if we did not earn our place. We are not here by chance or deception, but by the actions we've taken to deserve being here.

The *International Journal of Behavioral Science* denotes imposter syndrome as internalizing and owning your successes. Worse yet, simply succeeding more often does not remedy the problem, as the more achievements you claim, the more and more you can feel like a "fraud" just waiting to be found out. To see if you are suffering from this social anxiety, be sure to ask yourself questions like:

- Am I afraid of being "found out as a fraud"?
- Do I tend to be overly critical of every little mistake I make?
- Would I describe myself as overly sensitive to criticism?

And if you're answering yes more than no, it's time to start thinking constructively. My advice would be:

- **Take a realistic outlook** at your skill set—not how you *feel* you're doing or *think* you should be, but having an honest conversation with a mentor in your field who can objectively view what you bring to the table to get a better grasp on how to judge yourself. Then, ask them about their framework, how they came to the conclusion they did, and whenever feelings arise, refer back to that objective viewpoint to center yourself again.
- **Resist the urge to have "good vibes only,"** and embrace your emotions. We're not letting them overtake us, but allowing the thoughts through to deconstruct them and their validity. We all have bad days, and that release in de-stressing from one is helpful, rather than the harmful hide-it-away-so-it-doesn't-exist approach.

- **Seek out professional counseling,** since, as much as I try to help, a licensed professional is always more qualified for the case-by-case basis.

Unfortunately, in that Big House, it was only Sterling and me, and I ended up playing therapist.

"I'm not gonna tell you it's all in your head, Sterling. And I know you don't think I do, but I do know how that feels. At least a little. We both do, and we can't let them turn us against the other. There's no 'model minority' or one-per-campus quota, so there's room for us both at the top. And that's where we're heading, man. The top." I knelt down next him, on one knee and nudging his shoulder affectionately as he turned away in shame. "Don't play the comparison game. It's a whole lot like Monopoly: you can spend hours playing and by the end, nobody's happy."

This got a laugh out of him, if only for a moment.

"I didn't pull you in here to fight. Something else is goin' on," he admitted.

"Figured. What's up? What's got you like this? Did something go wrong with before?"

"No, no, you know we weren't actually gonna throw any bricks," he said. "We were just talkin' big, like we all do, y'know? Well, maybe not you, but where I grew up, ya had to talk big to get anything done. Just the way it was."

"Yeah, well, not here. 'Round these here parts," I said, dropping into a goofy accent. "'Round here we're honest folks, now ya see? So none of that there 'big city' talk, ya hear?"

"Oh, aye, aye cap'n." He responded in kind, a mock salute that breaks the tension in the room before he gets serious again. "I can trust you, right?"

"Pfft. C'mon."

"I'm serious. I know I asked ya before, about trust and loyalty, but this time... this time I really need ya to have my back."

A cold chill slithered up my spine, a dread forming but not quite there yet, and the body and mind knew not where to react.

"Okay," I said slowly. "But, ah, those two should be one and the same, right? No reason why we can't be honest and loyal?"

"...yeah, yeah, right. 'Course. It's just, I know it's gonna be hard to believe, but I really need ya to back me up on this."

"Gettin' a 'lil freaked out here."

"No, no, it's fine, it's fine. Just back me up alright?"

"Back you up on what?"

"Just trust me!"

"Why can't you tell me?"

Cooler heads would've heard the door jiggle, squeak, and then give way as the key found its way in lock and forced the mechanism open. But us? With steam coming out both our ears, we only saw the flown-open door, and the five fraternity members closing in. The fraternity president, the faculty adviser, and three other students, two underclassmen and a senior, pile into the room with a look of surprise.

And a hint of mistrust.

"Mr. Fenstermacher," the fraternity president says, in a manner to take control of the room. "Good to see you made it after all."

What the heck?

"What the—"

"Ah, ah," he cuts me off. "Ya know swearing's against the rules. One more word outta you and that'd been a dollar in the jar."

"I'm just a little confused what's going on here?" I asked.

The faculty adviser and president stand guarded and standoffish, defensive, even against the two of us, and the other students silently slink into surrounding chairs as if on cue. Something's definitely amiss, and the longer we awkwardly stand, the more a sinking feeling sits in the pit of my stomach that Sterling's fallen demeanor is not a coincidence.

"Your email? You didn't read it?" the president said. "Had all the details right in the folder. Of course, perhaps you've already been emotionally compromised to handle this case."

"I didn't tell him nothing!" Sterling says, so loud and sudden and forceful it reverberates in the small room, and the adviser steps in.

"I think it's best if you wait outside, Sterling. We'll call you when needed." And without another word, Sterling did as he was told, and I was more than a little beside myself.

"Okay, hold up, hold up, everyone just slow down. What is going on? What're we all doing here? And is this... this is the council you wanted me for? You said you wanted help with some unique perspective?"

"Objective reasoning," the adviser stated, and the president nodded alongside him. "The way you handled that little affair concerning the text messages was—well, it was commendable. We need someone like that for this. Though I have to warn you, before we go any further, you have to agree to confidentiality if you decide to stay. The proceedings tonight are under strict secrecy. No one knows until they have to know. Do you understand?"

I didn't.

"I do," I said.

"Then have a seat, and we'll tell you everything."

ON TRIAL & UNDER PRESSURE

———

"H-He didn't, did he? Y'all can't be serious right now?" I stammered. "The email said, I'm remembering, yeah, you wanted my help with creating a more inclusive environment—"

"A more fair process, I believe," the president said. "This is an internal matter. With a member in such high ranking and so high profile on campus, it would be near impossible to find an impartial panel. Nonetheless, we've located a notable representative from each year—"

"Making me your third-year rep," I realized.

"—who can remain objective about what comes next. Not only have you proven yourself, but you're also at an interesting crossroads in a cultural sense."

"I'm Black," I said, and then a visible shudder scuttled across their backs. "That's what you mean, right? You're here for Sterling, and thought it'd be smart to have at least one Black man on the deciding board?"

"Noah," warned the president. "We've brought you here to ensure an unprejudiced point of view for our proceedings."

"Nice choice of words," I countered, and the adviser stepped in.

"Enough, guys, come on. We're not here to fight. We're here to decide if Sterling should be kicked out of the org, effective immediately."

It was 7:45 p.m., the sun had just slid behind darkened clouds as crescent moon rose into its place, and within me, I too felt a shifting in perspective as my world turned over on its head while mine spun around to face the accusation.

"For what? We have any proof?" I demanded.

"We have the word and mangled face of a fellow member who claims Sterling beat him half to death with a stone. That's what we have." The president held my gaze. "That enough for you?"

I didn't know what to think.

Loyalty or honesty?

It was entirely possible Sterling was innocent. With no physical evidence, how could we convict? And yet, you have to understand, we were in the midst of a number of movements making massive societal changes. Me Too, Black Lives Matter, Time's Up, and our organization grappled with their relationships with these movements. We went in with the assumption that the accuser, the boy who brought up the crime with a battered face and bloodied stone, was speaking his truth. Go in with that presumption, and then handle the investigation from there.

As far as we knew, there were no witnesses, save for Sterling and "John Fraternity" himself. The event took place right outside the Big House, around back by the gravel parking lot, where Sterling had stepped out for a breath of fresh air. John Fraternity frequently used the back entrance to enter the Big House, on account of him coming from the south-facing side of campus, and it was more convenient to tackle the significant slope uphill by walking the gravel path than the often-muddied front way. This time, however, John Fraternity was running uphill, late for a meeting when he reached the back door, jiggled the handle, and found it unrelenting.

See, because of the high-profile nature of the organization, all doors required access from your student ID, a card everyone carried, and needed special modifications from campus security upon initiation into the organization. John had forgotten his card, and in his haste had barked an order to Sterling to *"open the damn door!"*

"Get it yourself," Sterling allegedly said without a backward glance. "Can't see I'm busy standing here?"

"Sorry, guess I should've known. You'd rather throw a rock through a window than use a door."

According to the record, John turned his back to the door, and that's the last thing he remembers before the assault.

All this was relayed through transcript—a piece of paper, not a person.

"Why not bring them in here? I wanna hear John's side of the story *verbatim* and Sterling's version of events," I demanded. "Otherwise, we're playing the he said/she said game, and I think we're all better than that."

"We already have John's side," said the upperclassman. "And I think he's in the hospital, right? So, like, he couldn't even give us anymore?"

"He went home," the adviser stepped in. "And says he has nothing more to add to his story. What's written is what he says happened, but you're right, Noah. We were going to bring Sterling in as soon as we all were on the same page. How're we all feeling about things so far?"

"...I don't think we should say yet," the first year piped. "You know, to keep us honest? Let's hear all the evidence first and then... debilitate? Is that the word?"

"Deliberate. And I totally agree," I said with some bass in my voice. "Let's bring in Sterling."

I hoped the baritone tones would bury the beating of my heart, hammering so hard and at such high speed I felt heat hurtling upward into lightheadedness, tightening my chest and tensing my muscles. A shaking, sweating worry washed over my dry mouth, and irritation inflamed itself into indigestion.

I'd never experienced the onset of an anxiety attack before.

The perceived threat of this situation sweltered and strangled my voice of reason. *What if Sterling wasn't asking for my trust but my silence?* A vote to convict, the removal from the organization, would take a unanimous vote lest there be an uproar about the decision. Everyone had to be on the same page, even as I frantically flipped through, searching for some surprise that would turn the tides in our favor. But was that objective? Or was I truly emotionally compromised? Would it be better if I stepped down? Or was my unique perspective the very reason I needed to be here, the devil's advocate among these angels of death to one man's career? Before I fell completely in this rabbit hole, I was pulled back to reality as Sterling sauntered in, a show of strength as he aggressively took a seat and stared down the strange faces that turned back to him.

"I didn't do this," he said, and refused to meet my eye. "It's BS. I'm even here. I'm here, tellin' you to believe me, and you won't even give that a try."

"That's exactly why we're here, Sterling. Just give us your side of things from the top and we'll go from there," the president said, and as he crossed his arms, Sterling obliged.

"So, I was out back, yeah? Just gettin' some air. I do it a lot. Bein' with a lot of these... people that don't look like me, talk like me, it's tiring, y'know? And everything with the group chat just set me on edge. What's the point of having me on here if we're going through the same things, over and over again? Gets ya down. So, I'm out there countin' the days to graduation when Di—"

"John Fraternity," the adviser interrupts.

"When this 'John Fraternity,' some punk underclassman comes flyin' up the road, kicking little rocks and dirt up as he runs on by. Doesn't say sorry, doesn't say anything till he gets to the door. Then he's bangin' away all, 'Lemme in! Lemme in! I'm late!' He turns back on me, like I'm some doorman, and demands I open that up for him. Y'know that plaque above the student life office? 'A lack of preparation on your part does not constitute an emergency on mine.' Didn't like the way he talked to me, so I let him sit on that for a bit.

"Next thing I know, he's kicking gravel at me, callin' me all sorts of slurs and sayin', 'Is it better if we say it to your face? Huh?' Picks up one of their bigger, jagged rocks, and starts waving it in my face askin', 'Was it this one? This the one you gonna throw through *our* window like a *thug*?'" He stopped and caught his breath, bravado breaking away.

The junior upperclassman asked, "Is that when you hit him?" And the fire was relit.

"Hell no! Forget all that. That's where he starts playing victim. I told him to get outta my face; he asked what would happen and told him something mommy and daddy couldn't pay to fix. Guy starts jumpin' around acting like he's gonna strike me and I get ready for a fight. If he wants it, he's gonna get it. This clown's half my size. If I did what y'all accused me of, there wouldn't be much of him left to cry about it."

"B-But if that's the case," the first year said, "then why'd he end up the way he did? If you didn't beat him, then who did?" And Sterling shrugged so quickly the crack of his back snapped across the table.

"Dude fell. I'm serious. He was jumpin' around, and we got out toward the front walkway, right? And it was still muddy from the night before so when he got out there, John just slipped downhill with the rock in his hand and really messed himself up, I guess. He got up and staggered off, so I didn't say anything; didn't think anything had to be said. Guy had a lot to say at first, got knocked down a peg or two, then walked off without saying nothing else. Seemed like he had some sense again, because that was the end of it... or so I thought."

"So you are saying you unequivocally, absolutely oppose the notion that you assaulted John Fraternity outside our fraternity residence with a stone taken from the gravel parking lot? And that, from your perspective, John Fraternity is at sole fault for what occurred that night?" the president asked Sterling, and Sterling responded in kind. "It's not my perspective. It's the truth," and then he turned toward me.

Honesty or loyalty?

That's when I let my best friend down.

ACADEMIC BURNOUT

"What's more likely here: that some kid stumbled down a hill and broke his own face, or that another fraternity member beat him half to death?" asked the senior. "People, listen to the facts. It just makes more sense that John Fraternity here's tellin' the truth."

"So, Sterling's lying?" the first year inquired. "I just... I don't know what to believe."

"It's tough, but we gotta make a decision, guys. We have to ask ourselves what good comes about from John Fraternity lying? Like, what does he have to gain from bringing Sterling down? It just doesn't make sense," the junior said.

All the while I sat, frozen in contemplation, an icy cool overtaking the heat I should have felt with an unfeeling frigidness.

"Gentlemen... it's been six hours," our Adviser noted. "We need to come to a decision, tonight. Now. It's difficult but it has to be done. What do we decide? Who here believes we move in favor of John Fraternity?"

The senior's hand jolted into the air, followed by the timider junior's, his face infused with exhaustion and anxiety. The first year, lost for words, finds no comfort here. Blank expressions meet his, masks of impartiality still half-worn on president and adviser, and the first year slumps back, with his head down, and his hand goes up.

All eyes were on me.

There's a reason we discuss mental health so passionately here. We can learn how to brand ourselves, the value of social capital, and to be functionally literate both on campus and in the wider world. We also let underrepresented students know of the systems that face them, and how best to confront them. As we learn, we grow, and before we can fully achieve a growth mindset, we must be secure in the sense of who we are. In that moment, I wasn't.

I thought about the branding I'd made, how that had become intertwined with Sterling, and, ashamedly, how the impact would reflect on us both. We had no evidence either way, no eyewitness account, and so were left to make a judgment call. I thought of the social capital amassed between the two of us and all the good we'd done and felt the twinge of self-preservation. If he was falling, could I pull him up, or would I fall down with him? I was literate on the culture of campus, the reactivity to events and the perceptions that were floating about. More importantly, I recognized when I voted, it was in more ways than one.

Honesty or loyalty?

And with one last raised hand, out snuffed the light of Sterling's campus career.

We all silently filed out into that early-morning atmosphere at 2:00 a.m. The moon looked down on us from above, and we staggered outward and homeward off on our different ways, nary a voice to be heard on a deathly-still campus. I watched my feet, surprised they were at Annalise's door, and I crumpled in as the door swung open. I barely felt myself hit her couch as she turned on a light and sat opposite of me, waiting. We've done this before, late night calls talking each other off cliffs and listening to long rants about the other's issues, but this? This hit different.

"I'm sorry," I said.

"Don't be, this is what friends are for," she replied.

"I know. And I know it's not fair to be here, keep you up at this hour."

"You know I'm a night owl. I never sleep. I mean, I do, but I can stay up with you. Obviously, it's all hit the fan."

"Think I'm the one that did that."

"Down on yourself again?"

"No, seriously, this time I've done it," I said. "This time... this time I messed up majorly. I... we kicked Sterling out of the org." Her eyes widened.

"Seriously? Like, he's done? That's it? Just out on the street? What did he do to warrant that?"

"There was this... I'm not really allowed to say."

"Sworn to secrecy, huh? Okay, well, it's a small campus, so how about I tell you what I've heard around, and you can just not say anything?"

"And how will that help?"

"Because I know you, Noah. I'm guessing you had to make a tough call tonight?"

I nodded.

"And that tough call involved Sterling?"

I turned away in shame.

"Noted. So you had to make a decision about Sterling in the org, and I'm guessing you didn't stick with him on this one? Must mean you either had damning evidence of what he supposedly did or..." She paused, and a look of sad understanding emerged. "Or you were put in an impossible situation where there *wasn't,* and you felt compelled to do what you felt was right in the moment. And you, knowing you, you're honest to a fault. You had doubts and you couldn't live with yourself knowing your loyalty impeded your honesty."

"Okay, okay," I said, standing and pacing as heart went racing. "I get it, you get me. You've always gotten me, alright? I just... don't know if that was the right call."

"Listen, you beat yourself up over a lot. And hey, maybe you're right, we all screw up sometimes. But it doesn't mean we give up. You eff up, you make it right. It's that simple. It's what you've always done, what you're gonna keep doing. You didn't get anyone expelled, just got them out of a pretty crappy environment, yeah?"

"...I should really call Sterling and explain—"

"Do you really think he's gonna want to talk *now?* Get that big head of yours on straight and then tell him everything. Everything, you hear?" she said with a playful jab, and I gave her one in turn. "You big softie. You wear your heart right on your sleeve where everyone can mess with it, but it's one of your best qualities and you know I love you for it."

"And I love you," I replied, with immediate regret, as her warmth evaporated and the shock sent her up off the couch. "I mean, I've said that before?"

"Yeah, yeah, I know," she said, though she rubbed her arm nervously. "And, like, you know I love you, Noah. You're one of the most important people to me and that's never gonna change, right? But, like, us...?" She opened her arms. "We can't ever change, see? The world... the world's kinda unfair like that."

"Whattya mean about the world? Forget the world, I'm talkin' about you and me." And it wasn't the time or place or appropriate way we should've had this conversation, but it was well under way and picking up steam as we're both standing and stammering, the emotions and justifications spilling out of us both and splayed all out in the open for once as my phone wouldn't stop buzzing.

"You and me? We're great," she said.

"So far, so good."

"And, like, I really do care about you, as more than a friend, yeah. But..."

"But?"

"Lemme just... but, it could never work out. We're great as we are, and I'd love to keep it that way." My phone vibrated again.

"A secret? Like you're ashamed? What, am I not smart enough or..." and I caught a glimpse of myself in the mirror behind her and it all became crystal clear.

She reached out, drew her hand back, started to speak, stopped, and then no one spoke for several seconds. Another screen alert sounded and I finally ripped it out of my pocket to see what sent shivers into my soul.

"Brother by bond, huh? Guess I know that's a lie now; you're a sellout. You sell out your own, and think you're better than us. You're not. You're not even one of us and you know it." The text was from Sterling along with an attachment—a link to some video shared from a friend of a friend on the web.

I clicked on it.

And I saw video proof of some kid walking by the Big House, pulling out their phone, and recording what looked like two college guys angrily, loudly talking, their barks incoherent over the phone's microphone, one tall and dark, the other, smaller and pale skinned, and the latter slipping on mud with rock in hand over a steep incline into a hard earthy fall.

"*There's your proof. Live with that,*" he typed, and then logged offline.

I didn't think I could.

"I don't think that," she said.

"But folks you care about do. And me? I'm just too big a culture shock to risk it for."

"Don't say that."

"Because it doesn't matter what I've done or what I accomplish. To some, it's *what* I am and not *who* that matters."

No response.

"So that's it, then. All for nothing. I'm not enough, Sterling wasn't, we're all just statistics waiting to happen, huh? What's the point of it all when there's no damn choice! I'm not the first in the family who 'made it' to college or the Black kid crossing color lines. No, everything defining about me was decided before I was even born."

"You don't mean that."

"I do. From day one. Hell, I'm adopted for a reason—"

"You don't know—"

"*I do!*" I finally snapped. "I've known for months. I reached out. Found 'em on Ancestry.com. I have a sister and three brothers. I was born in 1998. One of the brothers, he was born in '97. The other '96. I found them all, Ann."

"Oh my God," she said, with a mixture of anxiety and surprise. "That's... that's a lot all at once," Annalise admitted.

"And I find 'em, and they want *nothing* to do with me. Nothing. My own mother..." The words refused to come out.

"Noah... I... I don't know what to say."

"You can say, 'You're right, Noah. You weren't good enough to Sterling. You aren't good enough for me. You. Aren't. Enough.'" I took a breath.

"And you'd be right."

In school we learn that mistakes are bad, and we are punished for making them. Yet, if you look at the way humans are designed to learn, we learn by making mistakes. We learn to walk by falling down. If we never fell down, we would never walk.

ROBERT T. KIYOSAKI

THE SANCTITY
OF SELF-CARE

Annalise didn't deserve that.

Sterling deserved better.

These are moments of my mental breakdown, a series of events escalating throughout my time on campus finally coming to a head. Laying all your problems out on your friends, even your closest ones, isn't fair to either of you. She doesn't have the proper tools to manage this stress nor is it her responsibility to and putting her in such an unenviable spot is egregious on my part.

And Sterling getting steamrolled like he did was not uncommon either. Market Watch reports studies showing black students are four times more likely to be suspended from school than their white counterparts. A *Vox* article recounts US Department of Education's Office for Civil Rights statistics finding black students to be 25 percent of the suspended-kid population, despite only being 8 percent of the class.

Brian Banks would know, a then-high school footballer at Polytechnic High School when accused of an even worse assault by a fellow classmate. After almost six years in prison and another five years serving parole, Banks's truth was revealed when his accuser revealed she'd lied about the entire ordeal. The story was so moving it became a motion picture highlighting the injustices underrepresented students face.

Innocence projects across the nation set out to reverse these wrongs, citing disparities in school-based disciplinary actions, with a report from the National Center for Learning Disabilities finding Black students with disabilities approximately three times as likely to have out-of-school suspension or expulsion. The term **school-to-prison pipeline** may come to mind, and that's where these harsher consequences come from and add to a seeming prophecy that certain groups of students would do worse end up affecting their outcome.

In sociology, a self-fulfilling prophecy refers to the sensation best described as speaking something into existence, where one's strongly-held beliefs in an outcome ultimately affect events that factor into why it occurs. For example, remember my experience with the bigotry of low expectations? Imagine that, but tenfold, in classrooms across America. Continually telling certain underprivileged students they are not "statistically likely" to succeed, or that it is deemed more improbable for them while not offering any access or resources to fix them, only reinforces the idea of failure and further contributes to that outcome. A *Simply Psychology* article (Schaedig, 2020) describes two types of self-fulfilling prophecies:

- Self-imposed prophecies are when your expectations of yourself have an unconscious or conscious impact on your learned behavior.
- Other imposed prophecies are how others' perception of you can impact how you view yourself, and therefore, how you act.

The Pygmalion effect builds on this, essentially stating higher expectations can lead to higher performances in observed areas. The soft bigotry of low expectations creates an environment where underrepresented students feel they cannot succeed. Couple this with confusing an opportunity gap with an achievement gap, and you've got a vicious self-fulfilling prophecy in the school system. It is no wonder the American College Health Association found over 40 percent of students nationwide so depressed they have a difficult time focusing. Class can be stressful, but add these other factors on top of it, and you have academic burnout (Schaedig).

And it's not just across color lines. The American Psychological Association found, in 2019, 36 percent of college students are food insecure and over 33 percent have no stable housing. A 2018 study by the Department of Education's National Center for Education Statistics shows over 30 percent of first-generation college students drop out in their third year. Practicing self-care so as to properly deal with the mental workload you might be facing is crucial, and hopefully, you can avoid the kind of fallout I earned by not learning this sooner.

TIPS TO PRACTICE SELF-CARE

1. **Appropriate hours of sleep.** I know I'm bad at this one, but when you're already dealing with tons of stress, don't add to it by depriving your body of the needed time to rest and recuperate.
2. **Remain as active as you can.** Move it or lose it, they say, and having a soft routine that gets your up and about can help circulate some sense of productivity, especially

when it feels like everything else in your life is spiraling out of your control.

3. **Build your support system.** Leaning on them to the point that it goes sour is the wrong idea, so build strong relationships with your friends that you can depend on one another and give you that sense of camaraderie. Knowing you aren't alone in your struggle ensures a sense of hope throughout.

4. **Be wary of stressed-out symptoms**
   a. Chronic fatigue
   b. Trouble sleeping
   c. Loss of interest in pleasurable activities. In fact, to combat this,

5. **Engage in enjoyment.** Do what makes you happy, whether it be a guilty pleasure, a TV show, video gaming, writing, drawing, or some other passion that takes your mind off the weight of the world and allows you to breathe easier for a while. And of course,

6. **Don't be afraid to seek professional guidance.** I use the term "guidance" over "help" in this case because, if you're anything like me, you're not gonna call out for "help" so easily. You don't want to be the kind of person who seeks it out, and so the much easier-to-swallow "guidance" is used instead. Counselors well versed in helping the specific college student population you're in can help you come to terms with feelings and experiences that, up to this point, have been a mystery to you.

I know mine helped. Dr. Stacey Pearson-Wharton, who has been in higher education for more than twenty years, has assumed roles from resident assistant to assistant vice president. With a PhD in Counseling and Psychology from The Pennsylvania State University, she founded *Being the*

Dot, a podcast aimed at students and professionals of color surviving and thriving in white spaces.

She walked me through some questions concerning my own identity, handing me a job as a producer and a chance at working through these issues on my own, interviewing transracial adoptees like myself, caught between worlds: Black conservatives who thought a lot of this talk was nonsense and young, impressionable students who were still making their way and figuring it out for themselves. Maybe it's the new job, the national conversation around it, or me just wanting to get away from it all, but I wondered if our American perspective is the only one. If there wasn't something else to it in other areas of the world.

It was here where I gained some clarity on my situation.

You could build your personal brand, collect social capital, listen for the money, *and* practice self-care, but that wasn't enough. It wasn't enough because you could learn these finite skills, and after several podcast episodes we'd be left with a burning question:

"You point out what's wrong with the system on one hand and what we can do to course-correct on ours... but how do we know where to draw the line?"

I'd hate to point someone in the wrong direction, a self-fulfilling prophecy of explaining how screwed the school system is, discouraging folks from trying. Conversely, we cannot have anyone else go in blind, and end up blindsided by all the BS they may have to deal with. A balance must be struck, to know which errors to own, and others we cannot condone.

To defeat a self-defeating mentality, we need an ownership mindset, and that meant owning up to all we'd done before to move forward.

It'd end up with me stabbed in South Africa, but it was totally worth it.

5

"OWN UP" WITH AN OWNERSHIP MINDSET

THE DIVIDED STATES OF
MY CONSCIOUSNESS

———

"Education is one thing no one can take away from you."

A shining sliver of silver slashes my side, and as skin splatters open, I am reminded life *is* something that can be taken away, oh so quickly.

The blade bites through shirt and skin, its suddenness sending shockwaves through my body's nervous system. People panic, pushing and pulling one another as the boy with blood belching out of his side backs into the crowd. I stumble, stand, then slip down again, eating dark earth and fearing the crimson flashes that meet the cool blue of an approaching police siren, its screech canceled out by the screams.

A seven-hour setback separates Eastern Standard Time from the South African, where, in Cape Town, time keeps ticking, consciousness is fleeting, and the downtown district devolves into a dire situation. I can't help but think to myself, *some people learn by listening or reading, but I can definitely say, I learn by doing.*

And this *was* an educational field trip.

See, my undergraduate institution required me to study abroad for some measure of time. Most folks did it their junior year for fall or spring semester. Me? I took it over some summer break into the May semester going into my last year of college. This school, this life—it was something I wanted to get away from; I wasn't ready to own up to it all yet.

So I left.

Dulles International Airport in Virginia is where I'd last see my mom, who hugged me close and held back tears until I was safely on a South African Airways flight to Johannesburg. I was already straddled between a rock and a hard place: those being the window, hot as hell from the sunlight seeping in, and Tom, respectively. There were sixteen students stuffed into that steel cage, suspended in air, and the only two Black boys were, of course, quite close.

Physically, I mean, you can't decide where your seat is placed.

By this point, I didn't know him well, but knowing I'd be trapped with him for the next three weeks, I imagined I should break the ice sooner rather than later. Four sorority girls, the Sisters, snicker and snipe a few rows back, and some creative writing majors are already lost in literary worlds. Taking in the one or two oddball majors, a science one here, a psychology there, it's a pretty diverse group, except for when it came to race, which brings us back to Tom and me.

"Going to the Motherland!" he shouts, his gardener's hat still perched over sleepy eyes. "Partyin' it up in the home of our people."

We spent the first several hours traveling, on foot, through the grasslands.

It's strange to think I was once like that, so green and joyous and naïve to the complexities of it all. Out here, on another continent, I was so far removed from the Noah that was so broken and wanted an easy solution to his problems in America, that I pounced headlong into our walk to the Apartheid Museum.

For those who don't know, Apartheid refers to a time in South African history where institutionalized racial segregation was based around a political culture that praised white supremacy. Despite being the minority population through oppressive practices and policies, white South Africans retained the power and proximity to power until as late as the 1990s. For a frame of reference, *The Daily Show* host, Trevor Noah, describes how his childhood was dominated by apartheid ideology, with Noah famously recounting his mixed-race couple of parents being forced to walk on opposite sides of the street in public. This was the hall dedicated to all that had been reckoned with.

I thought I'd left my problems behind.

Our professor, a white Afrikaner himself strode up to me as I stared wordlessly at a park bench outside: WHITES ONLY.

"You okay?" he asked.

"No," I replied with a laugh. "But thanks for asking."

Our almost-twenty-some group piled into a revved-up van and drove from the museum to Bulungula where former South African President Nelson Mandela spent his childhood. Rolling hills of evergreen and a rich farmland spread over mountain tops, and modest huts belaying an immaculate home with gracious hosts. They fed, housed, and informed us on their leader's history, and I realized this was where Mandela stayed in retirement and was buried. Twenty-seven years in prison and released in 1990, our hosts remember his many mantras to live by. Chief among them?

I don't lose. I win, or I learn.

NELSON MANDELA

I think this over as our group throws themselves into laborious activity, the everyday know-how of life in their countryside. We herd cows and goats, collect firewood, and participate in the harvest. Monotony comes to my mind. There is a vitality here, a vibrancy that reverberates in your chest and puts vigor in the soul. This is a nation of people that have faced their past, grown, and become greater for it. I feel in me a resurgence of purpose as we move along, from elephant parks to Cape Town.

If you're still standing, have another beer! is proudly displayed over a bar's archway, and inside the shouting, singing, and somewhere-in-betweening that is slurring sways to the too-loud music. It's only day two and I'm at the bar, of all places. Keep in mind, I'm one of the babies of the group, one of the students not yet of legal drinking age. In Africa, though, everyone is drinking, and I order a nonalcoholic beverage from the bartender, Brighton.

He's got a magnetic aura about him, one not uncommon for his profession, as well as a wealth of knowledge on race relations here in Cape Town. He surveys the scene and makes sure no one's cup stays empty for long. In a way, it's reassuring: someone's got their eye out for you, and yet, shot after shot, I couldn't help but feel anxious by the attention. How long until the drinks, and by extension, our conversation, ends?

Do the two coincide?

I ask for another.

THE FLAWS OF A
FIXED MINDSET

———

"How's it different here? I mean, how is life different for you, as a person of color, here in Africa?" I press.

He relates stories of current political strife, and asks my opinion of the American President Trump. I answer, ask him how politics impact the people here, and he goes on to depict an internally-torn South Africa in the clutches of *reparations*. The very rich, very white plantation owners managing the very poor, very Black workers has resulted in a sociopolitical conflict wherein legal action may be taken, that action being the lawful repossession of land as means of "settling affairs" from the Apartheid era years prior.

The danger lies in that no one is sure when, or even if, their land will be taken.

The threat looms over many larger and old money-based plantations. Though, the general consensus I found in the very rich, very white folks in a country club we visited, was that race had very little to do with it, naturally. Ask them, and I did, and they'd reply people of color granted the jobs in menial work were still *working,* often given room and board on the work sites, and therefore were grateful to have said positions.

We'd visit these larger plantations, and it would be a stark contrast to the homestays in mud huts the group would also experience. The mud huts were populated with people of color, living their daily lives on the rolling hills by the beachside, collecting food, water, and other tasks necessary of their provincial life. Walk into the manor, nay, mansion, on the plantation, and you might mistake yourself to be on a movie set for a colonial American timepiece.

Make of that what you will.

Money was more than plentiful, with the extravagant decorations and ornate layout of the household, meticulously cleaned by staff, and the gap between classes had never been so great before. But Brighton still hadn't answered my question.

"What's it like being *Black* in Africa? Is it, like, the norm, or...?"

"Everything's about color, y'know, and people make a big deal of it. Everybody's just, like, shades of Black and brown and white and red and... you know, everything. Not Black and white. Then someone comes along and draws a line; says one's good and one's bad. One's rich and one's poor. Those lines that divide? That's the problem, man. Not the color of your skin, not the culture that raised you up. You get what I'm saying?"

I do, though the thought process is not shared by everyone in the bar that night, including an older, paler plantation owner with an axe to grind and a bone to pick.

"Don't have much of an opinion on it," he remarked. "Just feel as though... folks'll stay with their own, just out of... familiarity. No harm done—better that way, even."

But I've seen and felt the harm, and to travel so far to feel that again... no, not again. I'm fueled by that fire that needed feeding for the better part of a year.

"Well, with all due respect, sir," I go in, "it appears you *do* have an opinion on this. Suppose a Black man, say, like myself, were to marry into your family. What *exactly* would be your reaction towards this?"

He pauses a moment, thinking.

"I'd just as soon make sure you're from a good home. That's the problem, see. White families you know well enough, while others... not so much."

"So, again, let's play pretend, and say I'm from a good family, educated, hardworking, just the all around exemplary kind of man you'd want in the family. Would there still be any reservations about me?"

Another pause and then he floors me with his words.

"Just think about the kids, will ya? They'll have a foot in both worlds, never know where they belong."

Where *do* I belong?

There's a little Black boy out on memory lane who'd have liked an answer.

"And you think this... duality," I start, "this difference... you think this will follow them all their life?"

"Yes! That's it exactly. Damns them for life."

"Hopefully so," I replied. "Hopefully, they never lose that gift they've been given, that they appreciate the ability they've been given to see both sides of the coin. With more people like that I hope we can cross this barrier generations have kept apart."

He smiled, I remembered, with a genuine grin and replied:

"Maybe you're right. Maybe so."

Here are five whys to the root of the problem, and the place where you start to grow your mindset.

A **fixed mindset** refers to when we believe all traits and attributes are unchanging, that what we're born with is what we have, and that's all there is to it. Are you from a lower-income family? That's where you'll stay. Having trouble in math class? You always will. You can see how this mindset can negatively impact students. Heck, you can see how it negatively impacts adults. Education Week Research Center found 98 percent of teachers believe a growth mindset yields more positive results (Exclusive, 2018).

How can we fix it?

We start by changing our outlook.

HOW TO GROW
YOUR MINDSET

———

My green-thumbed readers understand that mighty oaks grow from the smallest of seeds, and take great time to do so. You won't wake up completely turned around, but there are some ways to jumpstart your own growing process.

1. **Change challenges to opportunities**: Do you know the kind of people that always complain, "It's a Monday, ugh!"? You're probably not picturing a happy person, are you? Turn the challenge that is Monday into an opportunity to get work done sooner for a possibly longer weekend.

2. **Reconstruct criticism as guidance**: As Mandela stated, "I don't lose; I win or I learn." Not all critiques are negative, and viewing them as helpful suggestions to be even better than before stops you from rejecting them so quickly out of hand.

3. **Prioritize the process over the result**: It's about the journey, not the destination, or more about how we get something done than just getting it done. Take your time, go slow, and understand the process before rushing to getting it done just to get it done.

Later, I realize I've had a little more than your typical drink per hour (but we'll keep that to ourselves). I also become acutely aware that, as the night drew on, I found myself taking out my wallet less and less often. Soon enough, it remained untouched in my pocket while my cup remained full. This continued from dusk till dawn near 3:00 a.m. where, in thick accent, Brighton declares the night over, and closes shop.

Tom is by now asleep, like most on this side of the world, when Brighton invites me back to his hut with this new group of friends I have made. As I go to stand, my legs wobble, my vision falters, and I begin to wonder if those nonalcoholics weren't so after all. As the others slink off into cabs headed for other nightlife spots, I'm behind one myself headed for a demonstration. Someone mentioned a protest earlier in the night, the lower classes rising up with all these new changes. I wanted in.

"You don't even know where you're going brotha," Brighton called, standing up while catching keys tossed from a friend. "You can't walk, and you wouldn't know where to go if you could. Come on, I will drive." And he helped me into the back of his beat-up taxi.

The demonstration was downtown, near the waterfront; a mass of people crowded the area while law enforcement barricades the excitement within their reach. I slipped in from a side alley and approach the action.

What's this for?" I said to no one in particular, *shouting* to be heard as muffled voices answer.

"What?" I asked.

"You're not from here." Another calls, and is there menace to it—or is that just the roar of the crowd around me? "Where you from?"

"No, not from here at all. I'm American."

The words slur forward, so slow and sluggish and yet so lightning fast compared to my stunted frontal lobe, alarms blaring at the bad decision made amidst an array of red flags. I'm paraphrasing, obviously, but it's not soon after I take note of this that the brain informs me I've been punctured by a long, sharp object.

I remember barely escaping, running from the protestors and police alike, daring not to get caught, and slipping away back into the hostel. Besides a little sickness the next morning, I'm surprised at the lack of blood. This all rattles through my head while in the hut, remembering South Africa for all it is. Beautiful exotic, and dangerous, it's hard not to romanticize it in the heat of the moment.

"Oh, hell," I said through gritted teeth, Brighton barreling down side alleys at high speed away from the sirens screeching away. Are they after us, or caught up in the confusion? "The hell was I thinking?"

"Not thinking much at all, if you ask me," he called from the front. "You're lucky to be alive."

"I'm, ugh, fine. 'Tis but a flesh wound," I said with a little laugh. "I dunno what I was even thinking back there. Couldn't have helped, but, like, felt pulled toward trying to do something when maybe should've... ugh... done nothing."

"A lesson learned. You *care* and this is good. But care too much for all things, and you see what happens. Learn when to do something and when to do nothing. Pick your battles, is that not what you say?"

"I should say it more often, it seems."

"Take on one battle at a time, little warrior man," he said, chuckling. "Go too fast for too long, take on too much, and you break. We don't want to see you break."

"That we don't."

"No."

I smiled, painfully. "That's pretty solid advice, my guy. I should start paying for life lessons from you." He pointed to this temple and said with a shake of his head, "All this? That's what remains after everything is forgotten from school."

"So, not a class we can take?"

"This is what they don't teach you in class. How to learn. How to *grow* from failures."

What they don't teach us...

And what if they did?

Through broken memories. I remember clambering out of the car, paying the man for less than he'd earned but all that I had, and slipping behind the key-coded gates of our stay. The next morning, I was surprised at the lack of blood. It's like a dream half-remembered. A painful one. With an ache and a groan, I was up and packing and ready to head for home when Tom excitedly popped by.

"Ready to go?" he asked.

I am.

"I am," I replied. And it's time to go; I had work to do.

I had some things to own up to.

See, what Brighton suggested was simple. Take each day, one at a time, incrementally building up over time to create exponential rewards. But he added on to this. And that's where he gripped me. We didn't learn this in school. And he's right. *Greater Good* magazine details how shifting our student mindsets can result in more practical outcomes. A 2007 study from the Society for Research in Child Development found that giving students study strategy lessons, the access to resources for change, wasn't nearly as effective without first employing a growth mindset message. The magazine offers a helpful acronym, GPS, standing for growth, purpose, and social.

To stimulate growth, remember:

- **It's less about intelligence and effort, and more about applying new ideas.** Talk of intelligence implies you're not smart enough to get it; an effort implies you're just not working hard enough. Instead, reframe this line of thinking, by reframing your approach to the problem. Really, this is just taking us from the non-helpful "just keep trying/try harder" to the more solutions focused "Okay, we tried that. What else can we do; what are our next steps?"

- **Gamify your education** through personal pacesetting and goalkeeping through game plans. By this I mean apply the concepts, often utilized in video games to the real world. For example, giving yourself experience points for the small tasks at hand, learning a new skill, completing homework, and studying can all be assigned values. What does this do? This emphasizes improvement and the incentive to keep at it. And hey, maybe every one thousand points or so you get a tasty reward.

- **Pursue problem-based learning objectives.** Prodigy.com, an educational site for online purposes, finds that plan of action reinforces long term knowledge retention. This places the problem at hand as priority, which emphasizes the subject matter—purpose—though this can really stand for practicality connecting the curriculum with real world application. No one wants to cram classwork just as scattered across a test later. We want to learn what's related to our fields of study. So finding what's related and linking that to what you do is important. Social refers to the fact that we can't do this alone. Build off what you've done and had before, and find mentors and allies in your classroom job who will provide immense help.

SELF-AUTHORSHIP THROUGH SELF-OWNERSHIP

———

It takes nearly half a day in the air to travel from South Africa to America—plenty of time to sort my thoughts on things. As we land, I shoot Sterling a text. *Hey. Listen. I want to apologize. Meet me on campus?*

I'm left on read. But he read it.

I'm sorry for... well, for everything that happened, I typed. *And I've got a lot more to say so would you mind just meeting me in person. I won't bother you again after this. I just have to make this right.*

An ellipsis stares back at me, three dots dancing away as he typed a response.

Why should I do anything for you?

You shouldn't, I sent back. *It's completely up to you. I'm seriously just trying to make amends, but if you don't want to talk, I totally get it. Just couldn't leave without trying to set things right.*

I knew he'd still be there. With what little clout he had left, Sterling still ran a mentorship program for younger students.

It used to have university backing. But that was before. The bus would drop all us study-abroad students off on campus where my car was parked. I would be heading home from there. I had to talk with Sterling before then. With only a semester left until I was out the door myself, this was a window of opportunity I couldn't pass up.

Fine. Meet me after my meeting here.

I knew where "here" was. We both did. He was referring to his favorite spot right by the riverbed—right where we first met. I wonder if he regrets that day. My pulse quickens with the spinning of the bus wheels, every turn taking me closer to confrontation, and owning up. I wasn't afraid of Sterling himself, but facing him? It would be facing down the personification of my biggest screw up in my life thus far. That's hard to stomach. An apology pounds in my head, preparing to pounce the second we're face to face.

It's takes hours and that's still not enough time.

As the sun starts its descent over the jewel-blue stream, Sterling passes over the hilltop to join me by the browned bank.

"Don't apologize to me. I can't take another half-assed 'I'm sorry,'" he said, walking up next to me without facing me. "You did what you thought was best, right? You're sorry. Really sorry. And to be honest? I believe you. But what good does it do to say it now?"

"It doesn't," I said. "At least, not in the grand scheme of things. But I'm taking ownership here. I was the deciding vote; *I* screwed up. If anybody's apologizing, I might as well start. It's the least I owe you."

"Definitely the least."

"Call it phase one of my giving-back process."

"Oh yeah?" He turned toward me now. "And what's phase two?"

"Working to make it right. With you. For others. There's a whole lotta folks who look like you and me from families as poor as yours and mine going through the same dang thing. 'Cept they don't have a clue how to go about any of this. Try to make some good outta all this bad."

"That's not bad, actually," he admitted.

"At least half good, right?" And to this he laughed.

"And just how are you gonna change the world, Mr. Fenstermacher?"

"I was thinking some sorta book? Like, a college prep book written especially for our kinda students. A book for us, *by* us, doling out the guidance we could've used a few years ago. Whattya think? Ya up for it?"

He snorted.

"I think my part in your story's done. I forgive you and all, but I can't forget when I needed ya most, ya weren't there, man. But hey, listen." There's emotion in his voice. "I've got all the faith in you. Tell your story, your way, and I hate to admit it, but people just might get inspired. Take some good outta all this."

"My story? All this? Not exactly a happy ending. I don't even know if I'd call it one."

"Who said it had to be? Maybe we need more stories like this, like us. We don't always get it right. That's not the point."

The point, the pain point, definitely needed to be addressed. What is the best way to positively influence underrepresented students, and give them the advice they need? Stories are just a creative means of conveying information, and all the best stories have conflict, the stories of our lives being no different.

And isn't that what is so unfair about it all, that most of us scratch the surface of somebody's story before making decisions about them? We are all so very diverse in background, experience, culture, and so many other ways, yet systemic oppression sometimes makes us view each other as competition instead of companions. We're realizing treating people fairly might mean treating them differently.

We understand with the numerous systemic issues facing students today, it isn't as easy as just telling them to "buck up." What we hope, though, is that they realize an ownership mentality is best exemplified as a version of the Serenity Prayer:

> *[We need the] courage to change what must be altered, serenity to accept what cannot be helped, and the insight to know the one from the other.*

Self-authorship through self-ownership is taking back the narrative control of your life story.

I was taking back control of mine.

"Where ya headin' now?" Sterling called out as I turned to leave.

"You're not the only thing I gotta own up to!" I said. "There's a little lady out there in need of an apology, too!"

THE PAIN POINT
APPROACH

———

American developmental psychologist Robert Kegan links **self-authorship** to the idea of internal evolution, self-improving through conscious, learned ideation. I build upon this premise and surmise self-authorship as the security of strength in one's self-identity. I proposed a problem-saving practice that could help students in need develop the skills they need to succeed (Morad, 2020).

Through personal branding, we understand how best to tell our story, on paper and in person. By collecting social capital, we ensure a smoother transition into these higher education spaces, and combine that with financial and cultural currency to better acclimate once we get on campus. Our mental health is prominent in our progression through school, and that means we need to effectively understand what is and is not in our control to stress over. While this book summarizes that, I created the **pain point approach** to do exactly that, and reverse-engineer your achievements.

If we want to change the perspective of diverse student populations, then we must start with our own wording.

There are systemic issues, absolutely, and while we want to strike down their structures at this very moment, we all know that's just not possible. Total reorganizing, while attractive, is not feasible at the moment, and I can't just wait until we "get it right" to do something. What I propose now is not to go against the notion of oppressive practices, but what we can do *in spite of them.*

We are not all vulnerable, helpless victims with nothing to offer. We have unfair advantages and competitive edges and can build our personal brand over time. We control what we can't control in the here and now, take ownership of that, and make our peace with what cannot currently be fixed.

Asset-based language takes us from negative to positive connotations. Common misconceptions surrounding first generation, nonwhite, and/or lower socioeconomic status (SES) students are *deficit-based*, or priming both mentor and mentee for the latter's failure due to factors beyond their control. As a rule of thumb, putting the person first is best. For example, it's not "a blind man" but "a man who is blind." The parking isn't "disabled," is it? No, it's *"accessible* parking" because it is made more accessible to those who need it.

As we pointed to before, there is sometimes talk of "underperforming" urban schools.

Try *underfunded.* Try *under-resourced.*

At risk is wrong—inaccurate. But it's not enough to just say, "that's wrong," because you know what comes next: "What's right?" Replace "at risk" with "at promise," like the *promise* of something more rather than the *risk* of something worse. These are shifts from a deficit-based mentality to an asset-based approach to education and life.

It's not an achievement gap but an opportunity gap due to lack of access and resources. Student success may look different from urban to rural schools, but that does not mean students aren't successful there. The Harvard Business Review found 25 percent of Black applicants got called back by "whitening" resumes. A resume can be "whitened" by removing signs such as a distinctive Black American or Asian name, and by removing work experience or naming volunteer work (or even entire activities) that gives out racial signs. Even being the product of a single-parent household or a nonnative English speaker can contribute to complications in the classroom and require reflection rather than a write-off. And by complications in the classroom, I mean:

- **Unfamiliarity with the college process and culture.** We're including the financial aid and application processes.
- **Lack of knowledge on resources** made available to them
- **Other external/internal factors.** We can't know each individual circumstance. Is one's family unit supportive? Do they have a home to go back to? What may be a given for one student is an anxiety-inducing uncertainty to another.

The goal of the pain point approach is to turn these traits into strengths.

- **Break generational norms**
- **Achieve something their family dreamed of**
- **Bring a unique perspective to a university**

All of the above can result in bettering themselves and their home communities. Their different outlook often results in some truly creative outside-the-box thinking for offering different solutions to issues and challenges.

Can they not speak English as their first language? Or can they better bridge the gap between native and nonnative speakers in an educational setting? Are they the first in the family to attend college? Or will they not be the last in the family to do so, and guide those after them with the knowledge gained today? It starts with the individual, but doesn't end there.

You see what we're doing here right? We're a addressing an issue that must be addressed in higher education by turning our weaknesses into strengths, or at the very least diminishing the harmful effect our weak spots have on our academic profile.

The "well-rounded" student has often been the one with a 4.0 GPA, plentiful volunteer experience abroad, and a job or internship in the field of study they wish to pursue. And hey, those are incredible goals to achieve—no doubt about that. The doubt does come in, though, when that's the *only* picture being painted. The student that has not one but two jobs to help support the family can utilize *that* experience to show work ethic, drive, and a sense of practical "street smarts" to complement their book smarts. That's called **transferable experience,** or bringing the skills you had from one position in life to another.

These are **lifestyle factors**: situational circumstances you are thrust into. Combine that with the aforementioned **intrinsic characteristics**—life course components you are born with that you had no control over, but have some control over your life's trajectory—and you may have some inherent conflict in your life story.

See, the pain point approach is just strategic storytelling, selling your skill set in an engaging fashion. Often, for underrepresented students, it is not that we are unmotivated or untalented (achievement gap), but that we do not have the same access and resources as our more privileged counterparts (opportunity gap). Through our asset-based approach, strengths, rather than weaknesses, are focused on and diversity of thought, culture, and traits have a positive net value.

In education, students can be valued for the perspectives and insight they bring to the classroom, rather than the areas of improvement. To put the pain point approach into action, every story you tell must have a beginning, middle, and end. Each has a conflict that must be resolved. The STAR Method of communicating information is as follows: Situation/Task, **A**ction, **R**esult. If answering an essay prompt or an interview question or giving an elevator pitch, this easy-to-follow technique keeps you on topic and on point with relevant information, trimming all the fat you don't need.

By answering any question/conflict/pain point with the STAR Method, you highlight transferable skills from one experience you've done to the hypothetical experience posited and your level of **competency.** Competencies are demonstrable skills and traits and are a lot of what you painstakingly describe in a resume and cover letter.

So, for example, if an interviewer asks about your past accomplishments and setbacks, you can use the STAR Method to answer with a mini story highlighting your active role in these achievements. If you are asked about your future, using SMART goals shows you have thought intimately about how you will accomplish these objectives. A 1990s study at the University of Konstanz in Germany found this form of if-then planning (for example, *if* it is 6:00 p.m., *then* I will start my hour-long study session) increased the completion rate of planned activities by over twofold (Lau, 2013).

So, *if* you are ready, *then* we can apply the pain point approach as a problem-solving strategy.

THE END OF ONE STORY

POINT ONE: PINPOINT THE POINT OF PAIN

Prior knowledge is important.

What are you bringing to the battle? If the point of pain for you is, "I don't have many AP classes or extracurriculars on file," what other experiences can you draw from? Know what you're up against. If you want a successful career and college is the key to cultivating it, calculate the odds of acceptance into an Ivy versus a state school. Which works better for your timetable?

Here, you should be setting up SMART goals, a concept created by the alleged "father of modern management," Peter Drucker, in his text *Management by Objectives*. He also posited the idea that **knowledge workers** were the professionals whose career capital relied primarily on set knowledge bases. Examples include:

- Architects
- Engineers
- Accountants
- Lawyers
- Academics

And by virtue of you going to college, that puts you in at least in the last category, which is further broken down into five distinct parts:

(S)pecific: Be well-defined and unambiguous in your ambitions.

(M)easurable: Make metrics for measuring your advancements.

(A)chievable: Ensure objectives are attainable and not impossible.

(R)elevant: Are your aspirations related to your drive?

(T)ime-based: Create a clear-cut schedule with start and end dates.

Point Two: Apply pressure to the pain point

This part, using self-questioning strategies, might hurt a bit, but that's why it's under the "pressure" sector. You're going to have to ask yourself the tough questions. What is it that holds me back? Is it something I can fix? If so, how? If I'm applying to a school with a legacy preference (parents attended college) as a first-generation applicant, what can I highlight on my academic profile to make me stand out? Use asset-based language, as always, but don't be in denial about the mountain you're set to climb. The five W's, essential for all information-gathering and problem-solving situations, are as follows:

(W)ho

(W)hat

(W)hen

(W)here

(W)hy

You can even add a sixth element, "how," to the list, though the focus should be on answering each question with incredible intricacy to lay out a comprehensive plan of attack.

None of these can be answered on a yes/no basis, so for each, you're forced to delve into the details of your objective. Who is involved in getting you to college? What do you hope to accomplish? Where would you hope to attain this degree, and why would you need it? Finally, you ask yourself how you're going to get from A to Z.

A general goal would be, "I want to pursue higher education."

A SMART goal amplified by the five W's would be, "I want to earn a Bachelor's in x at x University and get my application materials to them by x to do so."

I'm all about positive energy, but you can't climb Mount Everest in short-shorts and a heart full of hope. It's called the "death zone" up there for a reason. Be realistic. In the same regard, if you were the kind of student I was in high school with a... well, not a 4.0, understand the Ivy League might be out of your league this time around.

But there are schools besides Harvard and Yale. If the League only makes up eight institutions, that means the majority of folks *aren't* there, and there's nothing to be ashamed of in not going. Penn State, my big state school, is notable for being the second-most-CEO-producing school in the nation. A degree is a degree, whether from Cornell or community college, and it's way more about what you do with it then where you get it from.

These self-questioning strategies steer you towards structure over instability and can be honed in with the five whys for advanced appliers. Originally, Sakichi Toyoda, the "King of Japanese inventors" and founder of a little company you might know called Toyota Motor Corporation, applied the five whys to his manufacturing methodology to target the heart of any mechanical issues. This cause-and-effect analysis is really quite simple:

"I want to go to college." *Why?* "To get a degree." *Why?* "To get a good-paying job." *Why?* "To be able to afford the life I want." *Why?* "Because I want to be happy." While obviously the exact number of whys vary based on the situation, five typically gets at the root cause of the problem. Apply this to a pain point and you will break down a complexity to a simple solution.

POINT THREE: ANSWER AT THE ENDPOINT

We started with a question and now we come to our answer.

Pinpoint your past progressions, make a list, and then beside that, identify the strategies that succeeded. Were you creative? Innovative? Dedicated? A leader? Find out what worked the most, and begin applying that to other pain points that will arrive with some tried-and-true methods. By having an endpoint identified, you can also find mentors, others who've gone down the path you're starting on and can guide you through it more easily.

Firefighters don't just put out the flames and go home; they investigate, seek out the source, and ensure it doesn't flare up the second they pull away. Similarly, don't only seek to apply temporary solutions if the issue continues to arise. The goal of the process is to turn pain points into **pleasure points,** or when the "pain" of the point has not only been decreased but has been replaced by "pleasure" or opportunity for positive growth. Fierceton didn't just move past the follies of the foster care system; she actively worked toward solutions to those problems, and what once ailed her now aids in her lifelong mission that happened to help her earn the most competitive scholarship in the world.

This is a **storyline,** or a series of ideas that shape how you relay information. Maybe you best remember the story of

Mackenzie Fierceton, Tim Piazza, John Saunders, or even me. It's these pertinent passages that you'll recite to others as your takeaways from the book and the lessons learned throughout.

This is that story, *our* story, as you learn and add your own lived experience to it. For many, it's a case of the ill-informed misinforming the uninformed, and now we can break that cycle. When the story of your life gets hard, and it will, don't give up. Own up and turn that page.

I certainly did.

The next chapter of my life after graduating had me in graduate school, pursuing a master's degree in education. Sterling would go on a similar path of mentoring young students. Annalise and I would remain close. That college prep book idea would go through.

My relationship with my biological family would be strained, though the bond I had with my adoptive and found family and friends would strengthen over time. If anything, they inspire me to keep writing, improving, and lighting the way for others like me who maybe didn't have this kind of support.

Do you know why I keep using the metaphor of a story for guidance? Because, like our favorite books and movies, the best parts haven't happened yet, and we are the writers, self-authoring our own accomplishments. The pain point approach takes all that is against you and makes it work for you, giving you that competitive edge you've always had but maybe never knew how to utilize.

You define your personal brand.

You collect social capital.

You listen to the money that talks.

You make sure your mind is at peace.

And you own up to what you have to do to get to where you want to go.

Storytelling is one of the most versatile ways of exchanging information. While I made mistakes, I learned from them. While I succeeded, I could improve. Being a lower-income, nonwhite, and/or first-generation college student means coming into college with a slew of stories of your own hardships just to get there, but I hope this book guides and inspires you into this next chapter of your life.

The end of one story, after all, is the beginning of another.

We learn our most impactful lessons from stories. Before writing this book, I wondered how I could spin it all positively since most relationships break apart, circumstances change, and dreams are dashed. How could I create a happy ending?

I didn't. And this book is all the better for it.

Sterling and I don't make up. There's no hugging it out and then the dynamic duo's back at it again. The status quo has changed. The lesson? Not everything lasts; not every ending is happy. This doesn't make it any less necessary. Deal with failure now and embrace it, and you will learn not every endeavor embarked on is a successful enterprise. You can't ace every exam, attain every job opening, or even be accepted to every college. We teach folks to want to win, but not how—to desire victory, but not appreciate defeat.

And then there's Annalise. We **do** make up, but we **don't** get together. The guy doesn't get the girl. A failure? No—a lifelong friend. You don't lose; you win, or you learn. Not every goal we have is the one we're meant to accomplish but can put us on the path toward finding the one that is. If I hadn't made errors then, I couldn't help you avoid them now. Behind every wise man is a lifetime of mistakes he's learned from, which ensure you do not have to learn them the hard way yourself.

Understand the struggles that may lie ahead, but never let that define you. You are capable. You are worthy. And this is your time to shine. Prophecy is a powerful thing. Much like the elephants that learned helplessness, we too can become trapped in our own minds. Knowing what pain points preside and what best ways to alleviate pressure puts us in a much more advantageous position.

That's not to say there are not systemic factors beyond your control, but far from it. But I always advise to control what you can control and go from there. The last thing I'll write is my call to action to you:

Pick up that pen and apply the pain point approach to the problems your own life story.

And make it a page turner.

APPENDIX

—

INTRODUCTION

Abramson, Ashley. "What Is the Achievement Gap and What Can Educators Do About It?" *What Is the Achievement Gap and What Can Educators Do About It? | Rasmussen University.* (February 21, 2018). www.rasmussen.edu/degrees/education/blog/what-is-the-achievement-gap/.

Adichie, Chimamanda Ngozi. "Transcript of 'The Danger of a Single Story.'" Filmed October 2009 in New York, NY. TED Video, 13:10. www.ted.com/talks/chimamanda_ngozi_adichie_the_danger_of_a_single_story/transcript?language=en.

Hansen, Julianne. "James Baldwin." *Enotes.com*, Enotes.com, May 27, 2021. www.enotes.com/homework-help/james-baldwin-wrote-not-everything-that-is-faced-2630073.

Jacimovic, Darko. "30 Memorable First Generation College Student Statistics." *WhatToBecome*, March 30, 2021. whattobecome.com/blog/first-generation-college-student-statistics/.

Leaders, Thought. "Equity in Education: What It Is and Why It Matters." *Thinking Maps*, April 4, 2019. www.thinkingmaps. com/equity-education-matters/.

Ozio, Ron. "A 2021 Rhodes Scholar for Penn." *Penn Today*, School of Arts & Sciences, School of Social Policy & Practice, May 5, 2020, penntoday.upenn.edu/news/Penn-2021-Rhodes-Scholar-Mackenzie-Fierceton.

Sisolak, Paul. "20 Rich and Famous Community College Graduates." *HuffPost*, HuffPost, December 7, 2017. www.huffpost. com/entry/20-rich-and-famous-commun_b_7546150.

Writer, Staff. "Who Are Some Famous Rhodes Scholars?" *Reference*, IAC Publishing, March 28, 2020. www.reference.com/world-view/famous-rhodes-scholars-62e6c1a2a1fb02a.

ADVICE FROM THE EXPERTS

"Elizabeth Warren Quotes." BrainyQuote.com. BrainyMedia Inc, 2021. June 12, 2021. https://www.brainyquote.com/quotes/eliz-abeth_warren_690801

Fenstermacher, Noah. "Advice From Admissions Gurus."*1st Gen Class,* August 2, 2020. firstgenclass.school.blog/2020/08/02/advice-from-an-admissions-guru/.

Fenstermacher, Noah. "College Admissions Rep Answers 'Hardest Questions'." *1st Gen Class*, June 30, 2020. firstgenclass.school. blog/2020/06/30/college-admissions-rep-answers-hard-est-questions/.

Richardson, Will. "'College Readiness' versus 'Ready for College.'" *Modern Learners*, June 30, 2014. modernlearners.com/college-readiness-versus-ready-for-college/.

BIASED ON A TRUE STORY

Lockhart, P.R. "The Lawsuit against Harvard That Could Change Affirmative Action in College Admissions, Explained." *Vox*, Vox, October 18, 2018. www.vox.com/2018/10/18/17984108/harvard-asian-americans-affirmative-action-racial-discrimination.

Moody, Josh. "How the Coronavirus Is Pushing Colleges to Go Test-Optional." *U.S. News & World Report*, U.S. News & World Report, December 18, 2018. www.usnews.com/education/best-colleges/articles/how-the-coronavirus-is-pushing-colleges-to-go-test-optional.

Reilly, Katie. "What's Changed Since the College Admissions Scandal?" *Time*, Time, March 12, 2020. time.com/5801167/college-admissions-scandal-changes/.

Sahanya. "Netflix's 'Operation Varsity Blues' Sheds New Light on College Admissions Scandal." *The Vanderbilt Hustler*, March 20, 2021. vanderbilthustler.com/39221/featured/netflixs-operation-varsity-blues-sheds-new-light-on-college-admissions-scandal/.

THE FIVE FACTORS OF FORWARD MOMENTUM

Campbell, Japheth. "If You Don't Find a Way to Make Money While You Sleep, You Will Work until You Die." *Medium*,

Medium, June 27, 2019. yefeth.medium.com/if-you-dont-find-a-way-to-make-money-while-you-sleep-you-will-work-until-you-die-2484a56521bf.

THE STORY METHOD

"Bobby Womack Quotes." BrainyQuote.com. BrainyMedia Inc, 2021. June 12, 2021. https://www.brainyquote.com/quotes/bobby_womack_226463

Key, Keegan-Michael. *Mark Cuban: Power and Money. YouTube*, YouTube, February 17, 2020. www.youtube.com/watch?v=tM-RCHEw9aHU&ab_channel=BrainGames.

Maguire, April. "10 Famous Harvard Alumni You Need to Know About." *CollegeVine*, March 19, 2020. blog.collegevine.com/famous-harvard-alumni/.

Queen University of Charlotte. "Your Thoughts Become Your Destiny." *Stan Greenspon Center for Peace and Social Justice*, December 21, 2018. www.stangreensponcenter.org/2018/12/19/your-thoughts-become-your-destiny/.

Zafarris, Jess. "The Origins of the Phrase 'Pull Yourself Up By Your Bootstraps.'" *Useless Etymology*, November 7, 2019. uselessetymology.com/2019/11/07/the-origins-of-the-phrase-pull-yourself-up-by-your-bootstraps/.

THE KID WHO TALKS TO KLANSMEN

Klose, Jason. "The Edison Hotel: A Bright and Colorful History: Pennsylvania Center for the Book." *The Edison Hotel: A Bright and Colorful History | Pennsylvania Center for the Book*, 2009, pabook.libraries.psu.edu/literary-cultural-heritage-map-pa/ feature-articles/edison-hotel-bright-and-colorful-history.

"Robert Frost Quotes." BrainyQuote.com. BrainyMedia Inc, 2021. 12 June 2021. https://www.brainyquote.com/quotes/robert_ frost_101423

MORAL OF THE STORY

"Albert Einstein Quotes." BrainyQuote.com. BrainyMedia Inc. June 12, 2021. https://www.brainyquote.com/quotes/albert_ein-stein_38380.

Greene, Steve. "Chris Rock's First Standup Special in a Decade Is a Smaller, More Personal Return from an All-Time Great." *IndieWire*, IndieWire, February 14, 2018. www.indiew-ire.com/2018/02/chris-rock-netflix-tamborine-review-standup-1201928473/.

Hipes, Patrick. "Hilde Lysiak, The 12-Year-Old Journo Inspiration Of Apple TV Series, Strikes Again." *Deadline*, February 24, 2019. deadline.com/2019/02/hilde-lysiak-journalist-apple-se-ries-latest-scoop-1202563511/.

Summer Reading. "A Quote by Jeff Bezos." *Goodreads*, Goodreads, 2018, www.goodreads.com/quotes/7383200-your-brand-is-what-other-people-say-about-you-when.

LEAVING THE NEST

"What Is SQ3R? A Definition For Teachers And Students." *Teach-Thought*, February 22, 2021. www.teachthought.com/literacy/what-is-sq3r-definition-for-teachers/.

CIRCLES OF TRUST

Ordaz-Villegas, Gabriela, et al. "Development of an Academic Self Concept for Adolescents (ASCA) Scale." *Journal of Behavior, Health & Social Issues*, Elsevier, 21 Feb. 2015, www.sciencedirect.com/science/article/pii/S2007078013716924.

YOUR POSITIONALITY IN INTERSECTIONALITY

Elliott, Zetta. "Intersectionality & Positionality." *Zetta Elliott*, October 23, 2015. www.zettaelliott.com/intersectionalty-positionality/.

LEARNED HELPLESSNESS

Ackerman, M.A., Courtney E. "Learned Helplessness: Seligman's Theory of Depression (+ Cure)." *PositivePsychology.com*, March 4, 2021. positivepsychology.com/learned-helplessness-seligman-theory-depression-cure/.

Cherry, Kendra. "What Causes Learned Helplessness?" *Verywell Mind*, April 5, 2021. www.verywellmind.com/what-is-learned-helplessness-2795326.

Garber, J., & Hollon, S. D. (1980). Universal versus personal helplessness in depression: Belief in uncontrollability or incompe-

tence? *Journal of Abnormal Psychology, 89*(1), 56–66. https://doi.
org/10.1037/0021-843X.89.1.56

Wax, Amy L. "Some Truths About Black Disadvantage." *The Wall
Street Journal*, Dow Jones & Company, January 3, 2005. www.
wsj.com/articles/SB110471317183614902.

PROFIT IN YOUR POCKET

"Benjamin Franklin Quotes." BrainyQuote.com. BrainyMedia Inc,
2021. June 13, 2021. https://www.brainyquote.com/quotes/ben-
jamin_franklin_141119

Bryk, Anthony S, and Barbara Schneider. "Trust in Schools: A Core
Resource for School Reform." *Trust in Schools: A Core Resource
for School Reform - Educational Leadership*, March 2003, www.
ascd.org/publications/educational-leadership/mar03/vol60/
num06/Trust-in-Schools@-A-Core-Resource-for-School-Re-
form.aspx.

Citrin, Jim. *How to Get the Job When You Don't Have
the Experience*, August 11, 2014. www.linkedin.com/
pulse/20140811235043-203184238-how-to-overcome-the-per-
mission-paradox-you-can-t-get-the-job-without-the-experi-
ence-but-you-can-t-get-the-experience-without-the-job/.

Hayes, Adam. "What Is the Knowledge Economy?" *Investopedia*,
Investopedia, May 19, 2021. www.investopedia.com/terms/k/
knowledge-economy.asp.

Madda, Mary Jo. "For Students to Succeed, Social Capital Matter
Just as Much as Skills-Here's Why - EdSurge News." *EdSurge*,

EdSurge, January 10, 2019. www.edsurge.com/news/2019-01-09-for-students-to-succeed-social-capital-matter-just-as-much-as-skills-here-s-why.

Quey, Jason. "What Are Points of Parity? How Do Points of Parity Help My Startup Grow?" *Growth Ramp*, March 2, 2021. www.growthramp.io/articles/points-of-parity.

"What Does ROI Mean in Higher Education? - Best Value Schools." *BestValueSchools*, May 24, 2021. www.bestvalueschools.com/faq/what-does-roi-mean-in-higher-education/.

ACADEMIC ABUSE

"Reading Gilbert Ryle 'Knowing How and Knowing That'." *Philosophy Masters*, Scribd, January 15, 2012. philosophymasters.wordpress.com/2012/01/15/reading-gilbert-ryle-knowing-how-and-knowing-that/.

INTEREST OVER TIME

Claridge, Tristan. "Coleman on Social Capital – Rational-Choice Approach." *Social Capital Research*, 22 April 22, 2015. www.socialcapitalresearch.com/coleman-on-social-capital-rational-choice-approach/.

Claridge, Tristan. "Explanation of Types of Social Capital." *Social Capital Research*, February 11, 2013. www.socialcapitalresearch.com/explanation-types-social-capital/.

CNETTV, director. *Zuckerberg's Senate Hearing Highlights in 10 Minutes. YouTube,* YouTube, April 10, 2018. www.youtube.com/watch?v=EgI_KAkSyCw&ab_channel=CNET.

"Introduction to Social Exchange Theory in Social Work." *Online MSW Programs: A Comprehensive Directory of Accredited MSW Degrees,* 2U, Inc., July 2020, www.onlinemswprograms.com/social-work/theories/social-exchange-theory/.

Ostrov, Jamie. "The Development of Relational Aggression: The Role of Media Exposure." *American Psychological Association,* American Psychological Association, August, 2013. www.apa.org/science/about/psa/2013/07-08/relational-aggression.

Sienkiewicz, Emily. "Identifying Our Spheres of Influence as Change Agents of Equity, Language & Literacy." *Confianza,* Confianza, July 15, 2020. ellstudents.com/blogs/the-confianza-way/identifying-our-circle-of-influence-for-change-agents-of-equity-language-literacy.

Startup Info Team. "Dana Budzyn of UBDI Shares with Us Her Journey Towards Creating a Universal Basic Data Income ." *Startup.Info,* September 16, 2020. startup.info/dana-budzyn-ubdi/.

HOW TO MAKE MORE MONEY

Dickson, Paul. "Derek Bok Quote." *AZ Quotes,* August, 2007. www.azquotes.com/quote/30851.

Duncan, Jason. "10 Attributes That Require Zero Talent or Skill." *LinkedIn*, September 29, 2016. www.linkedin.com/pulse/10-attributes-require-zero-talent-skill-jason-duncan/.

THE MOMENTS THAT MAKE US

Fessler, Leah. "'You're No Genius': Her Father's Shutdowns Made Angela Duckworth a World Expert on Grit." *Quartz*, Quartz, March 26, 2018. qz.com/work/1233940/angela-duckworth-explains-grit-is-the-key-to-success-and-self-confidence/.

Hazing Prevention. "Hazing Prevention Home Page." *HazingPrevention.org*, 2021, hazingprevention.org/.

THE KINDS OF INCOME TO CASH IN BIG

Jack, Anthony. "On Diversity: Access Ain't Inclusion." Filmed June 2019 in New York, NY. TED video, 8:50. www.youtube.com/watch?v=j7w2Gv7ueOc&ab_channel=TEDxTalks.

HOW YOU CAN COLLECT CULTURAL CAPITAL

Alliance for Education Solutions. "School Culture and Climate." *AES Impact*, February 6, 2020. aesimpact.org/school-climate-and-culture/.

Bridges, PhD., Brian. "African Americans and College Education by the Numbers." *UNCF*, November 18, 2020. uncf.org/the-latest/african-americans-and-college-education-by-the-numbers.

Campus Carrier. "Students Deal with Homesickness during Their College Careers." *Vikingfusion.com*, October 15, 2020.

vikingfusion.com/2020/10/15/students-deal-with-homesickness-during-their-college-careers/.

Dedman, Ben. "Majority of College Students Experience Food Insecurity, Housing Insecurity, or Homelessness." *Association of American Colleges & Universities*, June 12, 2019. www.aacu.org/aacu-news/newsletter/majority-college-students-experience-food-insecurity-housing-insecurity-or.

Jacimovic, Dako. "30 Memorable First Generation College Student Statistics." *WhatToBecome*, March 30, 2020. whattobecome.com/blog/first-generation-college-student-statistics/.

TACKLING TOXIC POSITIVITY

Aristotle. "Inspirational Quotes at BrainyQuote." *BrainyQuote*, Xplore, 2015, www.brainyquote.com/.

Cherry, Kendra. "Why Toxic Positivity Can Be So Harmful." *Verywell Mind*, February 1, 2021. www.verywellmind.com/what-is-toxic-positivity-5093958.

Fenstermacher, Noah. "You Are Not an Imposter: 8 Min Read." *You Are Not an Imposter | 8 Min Read*, May 4, 2020. firstgenclass.school.blog/2020/04/23/you-are-not-an-imposter-8-min-read/.

Lukin, Konstantin. "Toxic Positivity: Don't Always Look on the Bright Side." *Psychology Today*, Sussex Publishers, August 1, 2019. www.psychologytoday.com/us/blog/the-man-cave/201908/toxic-positivity-dont-always-look-the-bright-side.

HOW TO PROVE YOU'RE NOT AN IMPOSTER

Sakulku, Jaruwan. "The Impostor Phenomenon." *The Journal of Behavioral Science*, 2011. so06.tci-thaijo.org/index.php/IJBS/article/view/521.

ACADEMIC BURNOUT

Robert Kiyosaki (2015). *"Rich Dad Poor Dad: What The Rich Teach Their Kids About Money That the Poor and Middle Class Do Not!"*, p.151, Robert Kiyosaki.

SANCTITY OF SELF-CARE

Arends, Brett. "Black Children Are More Likely to Be Disciplined than White Kids for the Same Behavior." *MarketWatch*, MarketWatch, October 16, 2019. www.marketwatch.com/story/black-children-are-more-likely-to-be-disciplined-than-white-kids-for-the-same-behavior-2019-10-16.

Flannery, Mary Ellen. "The School-to-Prison Pipeline: Time to Shut It Down." *NEA*, January 5, 2015. www.nea.org/advocating-for-change/new-from-nea/school-prison-pipeline-time-shut-it-down.

Kandel, Jason. "Woman Who Falsely Accused Brian Banks of Rape Ordered to Pay $2.6M." *NBC Los Angeles*, NBC Southern California, June 15, 2013. www.nbclosangeles.com/news/local/woman-falsely-accused-brian-banks-rape-ordered-to-pay-26m/1971672/.

Lopez, German. "Black Kids Are Way More Likely to Be Punished in School than White Kids, Study Finds." *Vox*, April 5, 2018.

www.vox.com/identities/2018/4/5/17199810/school-discipline-race-racism-gao.

Riddle, Travis, and Stacey Sinclair. "Racial Disparities in School-Based Disciplinary Actions Are Associated with County-Level Rates of Racial Bias." *PNAS*, National Academy of Sciences, April 23, 2019. www.pnas.org/content/116/17/8255.

Schaedig, Derek. "Self-Fulfilling Prophecy and The Pygmalion Effect: Simply Psychology." *Self-Fulfilling Prophecy and The Pygmalion Effect | Simply Psychology*, August 24, 2020. www.simplypsychology.org/self-fulfilling-prophecy.html.

U.S. Government Accountability. *K-12 Education: Discipline Disparities for Black Students, Boys, and Students with Disabilities*, April 10, 2018. www.gao.gov/products/gao-18-258.

THE DIVIDED STATES OF MY CONSCIOUSNESS

AIME, Philippe. "How to Win or Learn like Nelson Mandela, Rather than Simply Repeating Mistakes."

Medium, Medium, March 13, 2017. medium.com/@philippeAIME/how-to-win-or-learn-like-nelson-mandela-rather-than-simply-repeating-mistakes-2b4c45e33078.

Wong, Brittany. "This Is Why Elin Nordegren Is Not Your Average Celebrity Ex-Wife." *HuffPost*, HuffPost, May 12, 2014. www.huffpost.com/entry/elin-nordegren-_n_5310692.

THE FLAWS OF A FIXED MINDSET

Exclusive Survey Results. "Mindset in the Classroom: A National Study of K-12 Teachers." *Education Week*, July 26 2018. www.edweek.org/mindset-in-the-classroom-a-national-study-of-k-12-teachers.

Popova, Maria. "Fixed vs. Growth: The Two Basic Mindsets That Shape Our Lives." *Brain*, February 16, 2020. www.brainpickings.org/2014/01/29/carol-dweck-mindset/.

HOW TO GROW YOUR MINDSET

Briggs, Saga. "25 Ways to Develop a Growth Mindset." *InformED*, December 16, 2020. www.opencolleges.edu.au/informed/features/develop-a-growth-mindset/.

Ford, Hazelden Betty. "The Serenity Prayer and Twelve Step Recovery." *Hazelden Betty Ford Foundation*, October 15, 2018. www.hazeldenbettyford.org/articles/the-serenity-prayer.

Hulleman, Chris, and Larry Happel. "Three Mindset Shifts That Can Help Students Succeed." *Greater Good*, November 21, 2019. greatergood.berkeley.edu/article/item/three_mindset_shifts_that_can_help_students_succeed.

THE PAIN POINT APPROACH

Boogaard, Kat. "How to Use the STAR Interview Method to Get the Job." *The Muse*, The Muse, June 19, 2020. www.themuse.com/advice/star-interview-method.

Desai, Paru. "The Power of Asset-Based Language - Silicon Valley Social Venture Fund." *SV2*, December 18, 2020. www.sv2.org/the-power-of-asset-based-language/.

Hodge, David C., et al. "Engaged Learning: Enabling Self-Authorship and Effective Practice." *Association of American Colleges & Universities*, April 29, 2021. www.aacu.org/publications-research/periodicals/engaged-learning-enabling-self-authorship-and-effective-practice.

Lau, Edmond. "Make If-Then Plans to Get More Things Done." *The Effective Engineer*, August 7, 2013. www.effectiveengineer.com/blog/make-if-then-plans-to-get-more-things-done.

, Natali. "Part 2: How To Be An Adult -Kegan's Theory of Adult Development." *Medium*, Medium, April 23, 2020. medium.com/@NataliMorad/part-2-how-to-be-an-adult-kegans-theory-of-adult-development-ddf057b4517b.

Schwantes, Marcel. "Harvard Study Says Minority Job Candidates Are 'Whitening' Their Resumes When Looking for Jobs." *Inc.com*, Inc., April 11, 2019. www.inc.com/marcel-schwantes/why-minority-job-applicants-mask-their-race-identities-when-applying-for-jobs-according-to-this-harvard-study.html.

THE END OF ONE STORY

Hayes, Adam. "Management by Objectives (MBO)." *Investopedia*, Investopedia, June 10, 2021. www.investopedia.com/terms/m/management-by-objectives.asp.

Kudo, Masaaki, and Kazuyuki Okudaira. "The Lessons of Sakichi Toyoda Live On." *Nikkei Asia*, Nikkei Asia, February 19, 2017. asia.nikkei.com/Business/The-lessons-of-Sakichi-Toyoda-live-on.

Mejia, Zameena. "This School Is No. 2 for Graduating CEOs-and It's Not Harvard, MIT or Wharton." *CNBC*, CNBC, June 20, 2018. www.cnbc.com/2018/06/19/the-no-2-school-for-graduating-ceos-is-penn-state-not-harvard-or-mit.html.

Thoughtful Learning. "Check out This Minilesson: Asking and Answering the 5 W's and H Questions." *K*, November 6, 2015. k12.thoughtfullearning.com/minilesson/asking-and-answering-5-ws-and-h-questions.

Made in United States
North Haven, CT
04 October 2021